USING PERSONALITY
TO
INDIVIDUALIZE INSTRUCTION

USING PERSONALITY
TO
INDIVIDUALIZE INSTRUCTION

JAMES A. WAKEFIELD, JR.

EdITS publishers
SAN DIEGO, CALIFORNIA 92107

First Printing, January 1979

ISBN: 0-912736-21-6

Library of Congress catalog card number: 78-74138

TABLE OF CONTENTS

INTRODUCTION

There is a curious discrepancy in modern psychology, resembling the syndrome of split personality. On the one hand, experimental psychologists and other academic workers have succeeded in discovering interesting and important facts, and putting up far-reaching theories well supported by empirical data. On the other hand we have applied psychologists, working in education, psychiatry, criminology, social work, industry and other areas, who seem to rely more on commonsense, unproven Freudian hypotheses, or even largely disproved theories such as those underlying the Rorschach Test, without paying much attention to the scientific contributions of their more academic brethren. This surely is a curious phenomenon, unparalleled in the hard sciences!

There are of course several reasons for this state of affairs, and academic psychologists are by no means without blame. Having performed their experiments, and having enunciated their theories, they care little about the practical applications, and do not point out to the applied psychologist just how he could make use of these discoveries. It is well known in physics that something like fifty years elapses between a scientific discovery and its practical application; this in spite of the fact that in physics there is a large group of men (Edison is the obvious example) who mediate between the pure scientist and the applied engineer. In psychology such intermediaries unfortunately are largely lacking, and hence we have the unedifying spectacle of the divorce between pure and applied science in our field.

Dr. Wakefield's book shows just what can be done in order to bridge this gap, and to mediate practical applications of academic discoveries. We have been very much concerned with the elaboration of a scientifically viable system of personality description, including also the explication of causal factors. We have been at fault in not spelling out in detail how such a system could be used in education, in psychiatry, and in criminology. Dr. Wakefield has presented the do's and don'ts resulting from our work as far as they affect teachers, and parents also, in a clear, concise manner, not cluttered and over-complicated by theory. For those who want to follow up the academic rationale in detail he has provided the extra reading, but for all others who are mainly concerned with individual differences among their pupils, but don't know what exactly to do to help the children under their care, reading this book should prove extremely useful. We hope that teachers' training colleges will put this manuscript on their prescribed reading list - experienced teachers know perfectly well that all children are different, and require special treatment, but they receive little training in just how this desirable aim can be reached! This book will tell them.

H.J. Eysenck
S.B.G. Eysenck
Institute of Psychiatry,
University of London,
17th. May 1978.

CHAPTER 1:
INDIVIDUALIZING INSTRUCTION

Individualized instruction occurs when a teacher takes the particular characteristics of a student into account during instruction. The characteristics that may be taken into consideration are intelligence and previous learning; separate abilities such as auditory and visual processes; family, social, and ethnic background; and personality.

These characteristics may be considered in two general ways: (a) the teacher can try to change them or (b) procedures can be adopted to optimize the effects of these characteristics. Characteristics such as family background are not usually targets for change; instead, teachers modify their procedures for children from different backgrounds. On the other hand, previous learning usually is a target for change. Inadequate basic knowledge must be dealt with before presenting advanced work. The use of separate abilities to individualize instruction has usually involved both changing the characteristics and matching procedures to characteristics: a child's stronger abilities determine the most effective teaching procedures for the child, while the teacher also tries to improve weaker abilities through special training.

In educational settings, personality variables have usually been regarded as characteristics to be changed. The emphasis has been on eliminating emotional and behavioral *problems*, with very little attention being given to the different learning characteristics of children with markedly different personalities. The emphasis of this book is on identifying teaching and disciplinary techniques which are most effective with children displaying different behavioral patterns.

Applications of Psychology to Education

In order to consider individualized instruction in its current educational context, it should be noted that applications of psychology in education are of two general types. The first is the application of psychological techniques to all children indiscriminately. These techniques may reflect the influence of experimental psychology (reinforcement) or clinical psychology (unconditional positive regard). While they may be applied to an individual child, their proponents insist that they are better applied in the same manner to all children and that in this way they will be effective with all children. Of course, teachers' lives would be much easier if one technique could be applied universally to all children. Unfortunately, however, no current techniques appear to be uniformly effective with all children, although several may be used to advantage with large numbers of students. This type of application is very optimistic, implying that students treated similarly by their teacher will learn commensurately; for this reason such an approach is highly attractive to many teachers.

The second method of application requires that teachers take individual differences into account. For a large variety of reasons--heredity, early experience, nutrition, social and cultural differences--children are not all the same by the time a teacher sees them. More to the point, they react differently to the teacher and what the teacher does. By, say, a touch on the arm, some (many) students will be encouraged, others will be put off, and still others will take no notice. Techniques of this type are more difficult to apply, since they require the teacher to know each child as an individual and to treat each one differently. Further, this approach is less optimistic than the former. Even when the teacher treats each child in the way that will encourage that child to learn, there is no promise that the optimal levels of learning for each child will be the same. In fact, there are large differences in the amount children can learn and the time it takes them even under the best conditions.

Familiar applications of the latter kind have primarily involved cognitive differences (intelligence, cognitive and sensory abilities, or achievement) among children. Intelligence information allows the teacher to control the pace and level of instruction, so that the child is neither frustrated nor bored. The use of cognitive and sensory abilities allows the teacher to modify techniques for presenting information in order to take advantage of a child's strong abilities and develop weak ones. Achievement information allows the teacher to begin teaching at the most appropriate level for the child and to assess whether current material has been learned before going on to new material.

The Use of Personality Information

The approach presented in this book is of the latter kind. Differences in learning and behavior that are associated with personality differences will be considered. The teacher, psychologist, or counselor who employs this approach will have to consider a child's special characteristics carefully and treat that child differently from other children. While statements such as the preceding are often offered to teachers as cliches without content, this book provides a workable and coherent system for utilizing individual personality differences to modify teaching and disciplinary procedures in appropriate ways.

The material in this book is derived from experimental research into personality and learning as well as experimental research on teaching, school achievement, and classroom behavior. The recommendations presented are generally consistent with the results of this research. Although there are numerous contradictions in the research, an attempt has been made to present only the material with immediate practical application. Fine distinctions and unresolved theoretical disputes, although scientifically important, have been omitted unless they have immediate bearing on the use of this material. Readings have been listed at the end of each chapter to allow the reader to consider the original research in more detail. It is hoped that many readers will do so.

The use of personality information to individualize instruction complements the use of cognitive and background information to individualize instruction. Personality observations and questionnaires do not provide the teacher with information about what a child has previously learned in school, about strong and weak academic skills, or about how quickly that child will learn new material. Attitudes about school and expectations for school performance are strongly influenced by the child's home and cultural background. Personality information should be used along with, not in place of, these other important variables in planning instructional and disciplinary strategies appropriate for each child.

The use of personality variables should allow the teacher to use, more selectively and more effectively, approaches that were originally recommended for use with all children. Approaches such as mastery learning or discovery learning and techniques such as memorization, praise, punishment, and group projects, while not effective for all children, are highly effective for some. The use of personality data as suggested herein will not eliminate any of these approaches or techniques from the teacher's repertoire of instructional and disciplinary options. On the other hand, it will not—to the dismay of true believers in many camps—encourage the universal use of any technique or style of instruction. The use of personality variables (along with other individual differences) will require the predominant use of a certain set of techniques with a certain child to achieve objectives that, to some extent, are specific to that child

In order to individualize instruction effectively, a teacher must have a broad knowledge of different approaches and skill in applying them. The exclusive use of any of them should be avoided. When reading about, say, behavior modification, discovery learning, humanistic teaching, or whatever, the teacher may profitably skip over the obligatory every-other-approach-is-all-wrong chapter. Every other approach is all wrong for some children and all right for others. Only by considering personality, intellectual, and cultural differences among children can teachers and school psychologists decide which approach will be most profitable for each student. And, only when a teacher is skillful with a number of techniques will each student be allowed to work under conditions optimal for that student.

Personality-Treatment Interactions

The use of personality variables to individualize instruction as presented herein is consistent with the current search for, and application of, aptitude-treatment interactions (Cronbach & Snow, 1977). While most of the research in this area has focused on identifying cognitive variables in children that produce different responses to various treatments, some work has been done with personality variables.   As in aptitude-treatment interaction research, the central concern of this book is to identify subject variables (in this case, personality variables rather than cognitive aptitudes) that yield different effects under similar treatments.   In general, the teacher or researcher with this viewpoint will not try to change these subject variables directly, but rather will use them to identify treatments that will be maximally effective in terms of achievement and classroom behavior for each child. It is hoped that this book will provide the broad theoretical background for systematic studies of personality-treatment interactions in educational settings.

Since the research on which the material in this book is based is primarily, but not entirely, laboratory research, applied personality-treatment interaction research will necessarily qualify and modify the practical recommendations presented in the following chapters. While more precise recommendations concerning the use of personality to individualize instruction will undoubtedly be available in years to come, the present set of recommendations should both allow the immediate practical application of current information about personality influences on learning and behavior, and stimulate systematic personality-treatment research in educational settings.

Organization of Book

The rest of the book is organized as follows: Chapter 2 presents a personality theory evolved by Eysenck which has highly relevant implications for classroom procedures and has an extensive body of experimental literature to support its validity.   The next six chapters (3–8) deal with the three dimensions of Eysenck's theory. Each dimension is covered in two chapters: the first describes relevant theoretical and research findings for the dimension, and the second contains lists of practical recommendations to improve the learning and classroom behavior of students who are high or low on the dimension. Chapter 9 describes the use of the three personality dimensions in combination to individualize instruction and integrates the recommendations drawn from each dimension with additional suggestions and precautions for the use of all possible combinations of the three dimensions with all children, not merely with unusual or problem children. The final chapter (10) deals with the measurement and observation of the three personality dimensions and should therefore be useful to school psychologists who make formal recommendations concerning children, and who therefore require precise measurements. Teachers, however, should be able to apply the recommendations in this book based on careful informal observations of their students' behavior. In either case, familiarity with the behavioral variations along each of Eysenck's dimensions should enable teachers and psychologists to use personality information to advantage in the individualization of their instruction.

Readings for "Individualizing Instruction"
Blanco, R. F. *Prescriptions for children with learning and adjustment problems.* Springfield, IL: Thomas, 1972.

Charles, C. M. *Individualizing instruction.* St. Louis: Mosby, 1976.

Cronbach, L. J., & Snow, R. E. *Aptitudes and instructional methods.* New York: Wiley, 1977.

Dunn, R., & Dunn, K. *Educator's self-teaching guide to individualizing instructional programs.* West Nyack, NY: Parker, 1975.

Messick, S. *Individuality in learning.* San Francisco: Jossey-Bass, 1976.

CHAPTER 2: EYSENCK'S THREE DIMENSIONAL PERSONALITY THEORY

Eysenck (1967; Eysenck & Eysenck, 1976) has proposed three descriptive dimensions of personality.   They are called Extraversion-Introversion (E) Neuroticism (N), and Psychoticism (P).   These three personality dimensions along with dimensions of intelligence account for most psychological differences among people, and most of the differences that will be useful for individualizing the instruction of school children.

Dimensions of Personality

First we must describe what is meant by a dimension of individual differences. A dimension is simply a conceptual line on which we may place persons. For convenience, one end of the dimension is referred to as the high end and the other the low end, although we may or may not think that one end is better than another. Associated with each dimension is an observational system that allows people to be placed on the dimension. Consider the physical dimension, weight. We can draw a line (Fig. 2-1) and label one end of the line low scores (light) and the other end high scores (heavy). Using a set of scales, we can assign a number to any person and place him on the line.

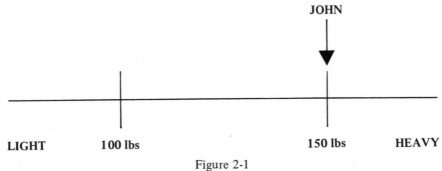

Figure 2-1
Weight Dimension

As with any dimension, one end of the weight dimension is not necessarily more valuable than the other. In fact, in different situations the value of heavy or light weight will vary. A football lineman, a wrestler, or a boxer will value heavy weight over light weight. Of course, above a certain point, additional weight becomes detrimental to these athletes—it is hard to carry and slows them down. On the other hand, jockeys prefer light weight, but not to the point of destroying their health.

A dimension, then, is simply a line along which people can be placed in order. There is no implication that people at one end are "better" than those at the other. Of course if the dimension is related to success in a wide variety of activities, it is hard to avoid thinking of one end as better. Such is the case with intelligence. It is hard to imagine a person being too high on the intelligence dimension in the same sense that a person can be too high on the weight dimension.

Eysenck's Three Personality Dimensions

The three dimensions under consideration are similarly conceptual lines along which people are ordered. The Extraversion-Introversion dimension (Fig. 2-2) places persons who are highly social and outgoing on one end (Extraverts) and those who are very reserved on the other end (Introverts). Most people are somewhere between these two extremes. It is not considered best to be at any particular place on this dimension. As we will see, persons at any point on this dimension will have strengths and weaknesses. An extremely extraverted person may be a good salesman and fun at parties, but he will probably have little patience with long periods of detailed, solitary work. On the other hand, an extremely introverted person may excel at solitary work, but probably would not do well as a salesman (Eysenck, 1967).

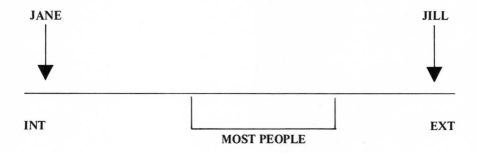

Figure 2-2
Extraversion-Introversion Dimension

The other two dimensions under consideration have abnormal sounding names—Neuroticism and Psychoticism. Since these names may hinder our discussion, equivalent (but more acceptable) names will sometimes be used—emotionality and toughmindedness. The neuroticism, or emotionality, dimension (Fig. 2-3) runs from high scores indicating highly emotional persons to low scores indicating very stable persons. Most people are fairly low on this dimension, although people with high scores are by no means rare. A person high on this dimension should not be thought of as "crazy" or referred to by any other pejorative term. These people simply worry more and have stronger reactions to stress and emotional situations than those who are low on this dimension (Eysenck, 1967).

STABLE
(LOW N)   MOST PEOPLE   EMOTIONAL
                                                          (HIGH N)

Figure 2-3
Neuroticism Dimension

The psychoticism, or toughmindedness, dimension (Fig. 2-4) runs from high scores indicating toughmindedness, aggression, and hostility to low scores indicating tendermindedness and no pronounced hostile or aggressive tendencies. As with the neuroticism dimension, most people are relatively low on the psychoticism dimension. Also, people high on psychoticism should not be thought of as "crazy." They will, however, be more aggressive and unemotional in their dealing with people, and their "behavior problems" will attract our attention more frequently than those who are lower on the dimension (Eysenck & Eysenck, 1976).

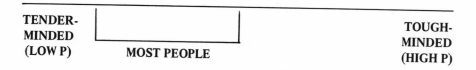

TENDER-
MINDED   TOUGH-
(LOW P)   MOST PEOPLE   MINDED
                                                          (HIGH P)

Figure 2-4
Psychoticism Dimension

Personality Dimensions and Behavior

Each of the three theoretical personality dimensions is a fairly high-order conceptualization of human behavior (Buss & Poley, 1976). At the most concrete level of human behavior, we observe specific responses, one at a time. If a person's behavior were described at this level, it would take a prohibitive amount of time and yield so much data that no one would have time to read it. Also, if we limit our thinking to specific responses, taken one at a time, the data would be useless in any practical application. We need to be able to predict responses in the future. Fortunately, a person's responses are arranged in reasonably orderly sets. A person is likely to give the same response to the same stimulus presented at different times and is also likely to give similar responses to similar, though not identical, stimuli. This consistency in behavior allows a degree of prediction and control over human behavior.

A person's behavior can be conceptualized at increasingly high levels until we reach the level of our three personality dimensions. A person who, in the past, has consistently shown complex sets of responses which we may call "sociable" to complex sets of stimuli which we usually call "other people" will probably continue to do so in the future unless through accident or design his behavior is changed.

The extraversion dimension is a general dimension that allows people's responses to other people to be communicated without voluminous detail. For instance, a person with a moderately high score on extraversion has usually been sociable in the past, although there may be a few people such a person does not like and is not sociable with. Also, sociability varies with the situation, so that a particular individual may be very outgoing at a party but much less outgoing in a large classroom. In general, however, this past behavior has been moderately extraverted and we may expect similar behavior in the future. Of course, it will be necessary to consider the situation the person is in when we try to predict behavior. Even with the information about the person's past behavior (extraversion) and the present situation, we will frequently not be able to predict behavior precisely. An example would be when an extraverted woman at a party, whom we could expect to be very sociable, was confronted with another person who had insulted her the day before.

On the same dimension, a person who is lower on extraversion has simply been less sociable in the past and can be expected to exhibit similar behavior in the future. Once again, situations and detailed information will modify our predictions of specific behaviors. However, the person's behavior, in general, along this dimension will not be surprising.

Similarly, the neuroticism and psychoticism dimensions permit us to characterize the general degree to which a person's past behavior has been emotional or aggressive and hostile. Persons high on neuroticism generally have been, and generally can be expected to be, highly emotional, although specific situations and other details will modify the person's behavior. Similarly, the generally aggressive (high psychoticism) person might not be aggressive when confronted with another individual who was obviously stronger, although that person may continue to be generally aggressive.

Independence of the Dimensions

The three dimensions are theoretically independent, although with certain measures and in certain populations there may be slight correlations among them (Eysenck & Eysenck, 1976). The statement that they are independent means that we cannot predict from one of the three to either of the other two dimensions. For instance, if we know that a person is highly extraverted, we do not know where that person will be on the neuroticism dimension or the psychoticism dimension. The highly extraverted person may be highly emotional or very stable, and may be very toughminded or very tenderminded.

The following figure (2-5) shows the three independent dimensions together (Wakefield et al., 1976). If we know a person's behavior with regard to all three dimensions, we may place that person at one point in the three-dimensional space. For instance, a person who is average on neuroticism and psychoticism and high on extraversion would be placed at point A. (Imagine the point to be behind the plane of the paper since the extraversion dimension goes into the paper). A person who is low on all three dimensions would be at point B, in front of the plane of the paper. A person who is average on all three dimensions would be at point C. A person can occupy any point in the figure, although there are more persons near the center of the figure than around the outer edges.

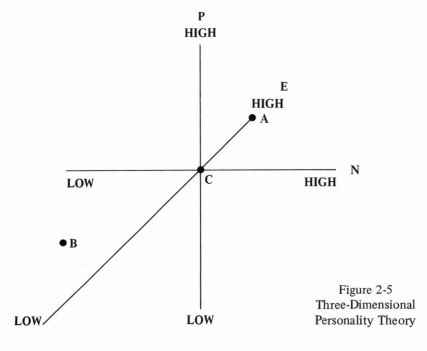

Figure 2-5
Three-Dimensional
Personality Theory

The independence of the three dimensions is counter to two notions in popular psychology. These misconceptions will be dealt with here. The first has to do with the relationship between extraversion and neuroticism. It is popularly assumed that persons who are reserved are also unhappy, emotional, and worried and that persons who are outgoing are happy and well adjusted. This popular assumption equates the extraversion and neuroticism dimensions. It also accounts for the behavior of a large number of people. As can be seen from the following figure (2-6), it is possible for a person to be both reserved (low E) and unhappy (high N). Point A represents such a person. The opposite, a person who is outgoing (high E) and happy (low N), is represented by point B. In fact, a dimension representing just this distinction has been widely discussed under the name Anxiety. It is certainly appropriate to describe person A as anxious and person B as non-anxious. However, this concept leaves out some possibilities—the person (C) who is reserved and happy and the person (D) who is outgoing and not happy. By omitting these possibilities, many people have come to think of introverted behavior and emotional problems as synonymous. They are not (Eysenck, 1967).

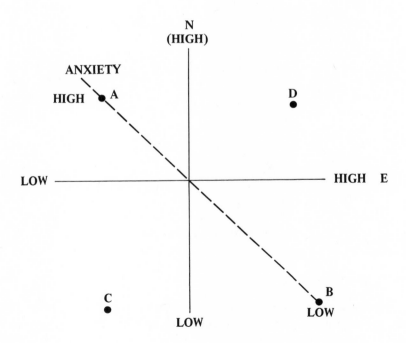

Figure 2-6
Extraversion and Neuroticism

The second misconception has to do with the relationship between neuroticism and psychoticism. Since both terms imply an abnormal dimension, it is tempting to think of psychotic disorders and neurotic disorders as simply varying in degree of severity. A good deal of research exists that demonstrates the separate nature of these disorders (Eysenck & Eysenck, 1976). It is not true that a person progresses from normal to neurotic to psychotic as has been thought. In fact, neurotics do not tend to become psychotics nor do they score high on tests designed to measure psychoticism. Similarly, psychotics usually have not been previously classified as neurotic, nor do they score higher on tests designed to measure neuroticism. From the following figure (2-7) it can be seen that it is possible to be highly psychotic but not neurotic (A), highly neurotic but not psychotic (B), neither neurotic nor psychotic (C), or both (D).

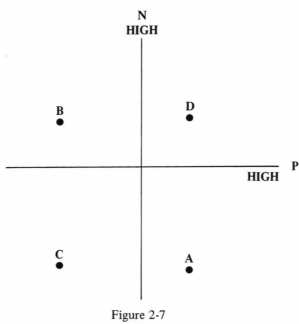

Figure 2-7
Neuroticism and Psychoticism

Personality and Intelligence

Not only are extraversion, neuroticism, and psychoticism virtually independent of each other, they are theoretically independent of intelligence (Eysenck, 1967; Eysenck & Eysenck, 1976). Intelligence is undoubtedly a variable of primary importance in school achievement and later performance, but it does not allow perfect prediction of school achievement (Naylor, 1972). Its primary use is to determine the level of difficulty and speed of the material to be presented to the child in school. Although tests of special abilities can be used to determine how a child is to be given information, general intelligence can be used only to determine what information to present and how fast to present it.

The independence of the three personality variables from intelligence make them good candidates for consideration in dealing with school children. Since they are theoretically unrelated to intelligence, they will not be redundant with it. On the other hand, these three variables should not be expected to predict school achievement as strongly as intelligence does, although we will see that some direct prediction is possible. Rather, these variables interact with intelligence and situational variables in producing school achievement. Considering these interactions provides information useful in determining how the child should be managed in the classroom and how information should be presented to the child to allow optimal achievement.

Just as it is possible for a person to show any combination of high or low extraversion and neuroticism, so it is possible for a person to show any combination of high or low intelligence and any of the other three dimensions. For instance, a person may be highly extraverted and highly intelligent, in which case such a person might be very enjoyable to talk with (unless, of course, the topic of conversation were too difficult to understand). A highly extraverted person might also have low intelligence. This person would seem very different from the first, and other people would certainly react differently to that person. Similarly, two highly neurotic or highly psychotic persons, one with high intelligence and one with low intelligence, would behave differently. Those with high intelligence might turn their tendencies toward worry or hostility to productive ends, while those with lesser intelligence might spend all their energy simply coping with their emotional or behavioral problems or in many cases find themselves institutionalized when they fail to cope (Eysenck & Eysenck, 1976).

Intelligence should never be overlooked when considering the three personality dimensions. Planning instructional or management strategies for a child based solely on personality variables can lead to absurdities. The teacher may reasonably decide to allow extraverted children to work in a small group on a class project. If, however, the levels of intelligence of the children in the group have been overlooked, the duller children will be ostracized, or simply relegated to inactivity, by the group. This result will defeat the teacher's purpose of combining academic work with social interaction.

The system of three personality dimensions plus intelligence becomes more complicated when we consider all four dimensions together. No attempt will be made to present a figure representing this system since it is impossible to represent four dimensions in the same figure. However, in using the system, we must remember that all four dimensions are to be considered simultaneously. We may find a child who is highly intelligent, low on extraversion, and average on the neuroticism and psychoticism dimensions. Another child might be low on intelligence, high on extraversion, and high on neuroticism and psychoticism. Appropriate instruction and management for these two children would be very different—the first requiring primarily independent work at a fairly high level and the second requiring a good deal of group interaction, less demanding work, and a considerable amount of encouragement and control of behavior problems. Since the four dimensions are theoretically independent, any combination of them may be found in one child, and all combinations will be found in a heterogeneous school.

Misconceptions concerning the relationships between intelligence and personality have developed. There is a popular notion that intelligence and introversion go together. Although there is a limited degree of truth to this notion at advanced educational levels, in general, intelligence and the extraversion dimension are approximately independent. There are children who fit the popular stereotype, that is, they are highly intelligent and introverted or low on intelligence and extraverted. There are also children who are intelligent and extraverted as well as those who are low in intelligence and introverted (Eysenck, 1967).

A second misconception is that highly intelligent people are maladjusted (i.e., highly neurotic). This notion is contrary to fact. Research shows that highly intelligent people tend to be somewhat better adjusted than others. However, since the theoretical dimension of neuroticism is independent of intelligence, and since we actually find some highly intelligent people who are high on neuroticism and some who are low on neuroticism, we will treat neuroticism and intelligence as independent dimensions. It should also be noted that persons with low intelligence may be either high or low on neuroticism (Eysenck, 1967).

The third misconception involves the image of the "mad scientist," who would be a person high in intelligence and high on psychoticism. Fortunately, most people probably do not take this image as a general state of affairs. Although persons high in intelligence and high on psychoticism do exist, intelligence is actually somewhat negatively related to psychoticism. However, since we find persons showing all combinations of high and low intelligence and high and low psychoticism, we will treat these dimensions as independent (Eysenck & Eysenck, 1976).

Summary

A personality theory consisting of three broad dimensions of behavior was described. The three dimensions—Extraversion, Neuroticism, and Psychoticism—are independent of each other and independent of intelligence. Using these dimensions allows a psychologist to describe the broad characteristics of a person's behavior. These characteristics will be taken into account in planning instructional and disciplinary strategies in the following chapters.

Readings for "Eysenck's Personality Theory"
Brody, N. *Personality: Research and theory.* New York: Academic Press, 1972.
Buss, A. R., & Poley, W. *Individual differences: Traits and factors.* New York: Wiley, 1976.
Eysenck, H. J. *The biological basis of personality.* Springfield, IL: Thomas, 1967.

Eysenck, H. J. *Handbook of abnormal psychology*. San Diego: EdITS, 1973.

Eysenck, H. J. (Ed.). *The measurement of personality*. Baltimore: University Park Press, 1976.

Eysenck, H. J., & Eysenck, S. B. G. *Psychoticism as a dimension of personality*. London: Hodder & Stoughton, 1976.

Eysenck, H. J., & Wilson, G. *Know your own personality*. New York: Barnes & Noble, 1976.

Naylor, F. D. *Personality and educational achievement*. Sydney: Wiley, 1972.

Wakefield, J. A., Jr., Yom, B. L., Bradley, P. E., Doughtie, E. B., Cox, J. A., & Kraft, I. A. Eysenck's .personality dimensions: A model for the MMPI. In H. J. Eysenck (Ed.), *The measurement of personality*. Baltimore: University Park Press, 1976, pp. 36-43.

CHAPTER 3:
EXTRAVERSION – INTROVERSION

The following two chapters (3 & 4) deal with Extraversion-Introversion. Chapter 3 contains an overview of the characteristics along this dimension that are relevant to teaching. Chapter 4 contains practical recommendations for teaching students who are extraverted or introverted.

Extraversion-Introversion is one of the most widely discussed personality dimensions. It is central in the work of Eysenck and Cattell, and important, although in a somewhat different form, in the work of Guilford, all of whom have inspired most of the theoretically based measures of personality. Extraversion scales appear on virtually all major personality tests, and it enters (formally or otherwise) into the treatment of most adults and children with adjustment and learning problems (cf. Buss & Poley, 1976).

A person's level of extraversion is probably the first characteristic noticed by others; in fact, this characteristic determines the degree to which a person is noticed by others in the first place. When asked to describe a person, we produce words such as "shy, withdrawn, and quiet" or "friendly, loud, and outgoing" very early. Of course, if the person we are trying to describe is very close to average on those traits, we will probably not bother to mention it. This is true of any trait: we are more likely to consider a person's extreme qualities as containing more information than those qualities which are average.

Definition

Eysenck describes extraverts and introverts as follows:

The typical extravert is sociable, likes parties, has many friends, needs to have people to talk to, and does not like reading or studying by himself. He craves excitement, takes chances, often sticks his neck out, acts on the spur of the moment and is generally an impulsive individual. He is fond of practical jokes, always has a ready answer, and generally likes change. He is carefree, easy-going, optimistic, and likes to "laugh and be merry." He prefers to keep moving and doing things, tends to be aggressive, and to lose

16

his temper quickly. His feelings are not kept under tight control, and he is not always a reliable person.

The typical introvert is a quiet, retiring sort of person, introspective, fond of books rather than people; he is reserved and distant except to intimate friends. He tends to plan ahead, "looks before he leaps," and distrusts the impulse of the moment. He does not like excitement, takes matters of everyday life with proper seriousness, and likes a well-ordered mode of life. He keeps his feelings under close control, seldom behaves in an aggressive manner, and does not lose his temper easily. He is reliable, somewhat pessimistic, and places great value on ethical standards. (Eysenck & Eysenck, 1975, p. 5).

The word ambivert is commonly used for those who are intermediate between the two extremes. Ambivert is a better word for these people than, say, "normal," since the entire range of extraversion-introversion is usually considered normal. Extreme extraverts or introverts are not usually thought to need treatment for this reason alone, although they are thought to develop different types of abnormal behavior in response to similar environmental factors or in combination with similar levels of other personality traits (Eysenck, 1967).

Extraversion and Behavior

The two most characteristic differences between extreme extraverts and extreme introverts are their degrees of sociability and impulsivity (Eysenck, 1967). A highly extraverted person tends to seek out people and enjoys their company. The introverted person avoids people and is socially uncomfortable in their presence, especially when the person is the center of attention. Also, the extraverted person tends to say and do the first thing that comes to mind. Depending on the situation, this tendency may enhance social interaction or lead to embarrassment. The introverted person, on the other hand, is inhibited. The consequences of actions and statements are thought through carefully before saying or doing anything. Many of the things such a person thinks of doing or saying may be inhibited because they may have negative consequences.

The different approaches extreme introverts and extraverts take to work situations are important. The more extraverted person usually works more quickly than introverted persons. In fact, the extravert may seem to sacrifice accuracy for speed, making more errors than introverts. The introverted person, on the other hand, sacrifices speed for accuracy. The introvert works slowly, but makes few mistakes. This difference is consistent with the extravert's tendency to be impulsive and the introvert's tendency to consider behavior carefully before acting (Eysenck, 1967).

The introverted person usually seems to be more highly motivated to perform well in a variety of tasks than does the extraverted person. Such a person reports higher levels of aspiration than the extraverted person, and will tend to persist longer at a task than the extraverted person. The introverted person will maintain attention on tasks for long periods, while the extraverted person will require relatively frequent breaks and changes of activity (Eysenck, 1967).

Extraversion and Arousal

While the introverted person seems more motivated to perform well than the extraverted person, the use of external stress to increase motivation has different results for the two extremes.   External stress usually improves the performance of extraverts and impairs the performance of introverts.   The theoretical explanation for this difference involves three statements concerning the person's level of arousal.   First, introverted persons are more aroused in general.   Second, arousal enhances performance only up to a certain (intermediate) level—a person who is too little aroused will not try very hard, while one who is too highly aroused will be too rigid, cautious, and nervous to perform as well as he might.   Third, external stress raises a person's arousal level. Therefore, with a relatively unaroused extravert, external stress raises the arousal level, resulting in improved performance.   With the already aroused introvert, external stress pushes the arousal level past the optimal point and results in poorer performance (Eysenck, 1967; M. Eysenck, 1976).

The following figure (3-1) illustrates the relationship between arousal and performance (cf. Eysenck, 1976).   Point A_1 represents the initial arousal level of an extraverted person.   Arousal level is low and the quality of performance on some tasks is intermediate.   If the arousal level is raised by means of external stress, performance should improve (point A_2).   Point B_1 represents the initial arousal level of an introverted person.   Arousal level is high and the quality of performance on some tasks is intermediate.   If the arousal level is raised by means of external stress, performance will probably become worse (point B_2).

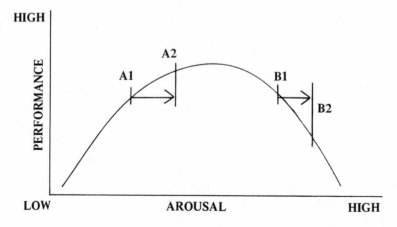

Figure 3-1
Arousal and Performance

In fact, improving the performance of this person would require lowering arousal level. We might accomplish this by deemphasizing the importance of the task or training the person to relax before beginning the task.

Two other factors must be taken into account when considering the use of external stress with introverts and extraverts. The first factor is the person's level of neuroticism. This variable also influences arousal and is related to task performance. Since neuroticism will be discussed in the next chapter, we will not consider it further here (cf. Eysenck, 1976).

The second factor is the difficulty of the task. Task difficulty influences the optimal arousal level—the easier the task, the higher the optimal arousal level. For a very easy task (that is, easy for the person doing it), the optimal arousal level is extremely high, possibly higher than the initial arousal level of any person, introvert of extravert. For very difficult tasks the optimal arousal level is very low, possibly lower than anyone's initial arousal level. In fact, there are reports of solutions being found to extremely difficult problems during sleep, a state of extremely low arousal (e.g., Kekule's discovery of the benzine ring). For very difficult problems, efforts should be made to have everyone (introverted or extraverted) as relaxed as possible (Eysenck, 1967).

Extraversion and Learning

Two characteristics of learning vary with extraversion-introversion. The first is rate of conditioning. Under certain conditions, introverts learn (condition) more quickly than extraverts. These conditions include (a) weak stimuli, (b) partial (rather than continuous) reinforcement, and (c) short intervals between stimuli that are to be associated. To the extent that these conditions describe a classroom, introverts will have an advantage over extraverts. Where these conditions are reversed, introverts have no advantage, and may even be at a disadvantage (Eysenck, 1967).

The differences in learning between introverts and extraverts mean that exactly the same sequence of lessons will be learned differently by two learners. The extraverted learner will learn the major points, i.e., those that are strongly presented, but will not learn the minor (weak) points as well as the introverted learner. Similarly, the extraverted learner will learn when reinforcement (or feedback) is given after every trial, whereas the introverted learner will perform well with only occasional feedback. Both the above differences make the learning of the extravert seem more general, and that of the introvert, more detailed.

One advantage the extravert may have is in associating concepts presented at different times, that is, with a long interval between the stimuli. This may result in the learner's learning things the teacher had not intended to teach. In moderation, this tendency may be judged "creative," although it may make the student's work seem disjointed if not encouraged to explain clearly where the information came from and how it is related.

Another advantage extraverts have has been referred to as "reminiscence"

(Eysenck, 1967). Reminiscence refers to a person's performance on a learned task, say a list of memorized words, improving after a rest period during which there is no practice on the task. Reminiscence is characteristic of extraverts. A short rest period after practicing a task will often result in imporved perform-ance for highly extraverted persons, while the introvert's performance is usually at its best immediately after learning. The reminiscence effect allows the extra-verted person an advantage in recalling information after a short interval (about 5 minutes). However, for longer intervals introverted persons have better memory.

It has been observed that extraverts achieve more in school than introverts up to the age of about 13 or 14 years (Entwistle, 1972; Honess & Kline, 1974; Naylor, 1972). From that point on, introverts achieve more than extraverts. A possible explanation for this observation is that the conditions in the early grades favor extraverts while those in the more advanced grades favor introverts. It seems reasonable that extraverts would perform well in the elementary class which typically allows a good deal of individual attention, continuous feedback, group work, and short lessons. Instruction in high school tends to be more impersonal, requiring longer periods of studying alone and greater attention to detailed work (i.e., weakly presented stimuli), which are conditions favoring the more introverted students.

Extraversion and Discipline

Gray (1973) has proposed a theory to explain differences in extraversion and neuroticism. The part of the theory concerning neuroticism will be discussed later. With regard to the extraversion dimension, Gray points out that sensitivity to rewards and sensitivity to threats of punishment vary on this dimension. Although both reward and punishment are effective to some degree with both introverts and extraverts, introverts are more sensitive to punishment and extra-verts are more sensitive to reward. Thus, the extraverted person's behavior is primarily directed toward obtaining rewards, and the introverted person's behavior is primarily directed toward avoiding punishment. In dealing with these two extremes, the teacher can control the behavior of extraverts better with rewards and the behavior of introverts better with threats of punishment.

It is not suggested that the teacher always punish introverts and reward extra-verts. Several reasons for avoiding this extreme application of Gray's theory are apparent. First, if one student is consistently punished (or threatened with punishment) and another is consistently rewarded, the first will see the teacher's behavior as unfair. Feelings of resentment will probably result in lower academic achievement. Second, the overuse of either of these techniques (reward or punishment) seems to weaken its effects (cf., Brophy & Evertson, 1976). Third, strong threats of punishment or the actual administration of punishment will increase the student's arousal level resulting in decreased per-formance by introverted students and (possibly) increased performance by extraverted students. This last statement may seem to contradict Gray's theory, but it really does not. The introverted student is primarily oriented toward avoiding punishment; however, the strong stimulus of actual (or loudly threatened) punishment makes such students less effective at avoiding it.

The practical use of the different sensitivity of extraverts and introverts to reward and punishment requires the teacher to make relatively small shifts in emphasis for the different students in the class. The teacher has a fairly wide range of positive and negative experiences that can be made contingent on the students' behaviors. Free time, and doing favorite activities, or extra time on disliked activities, and a phone call to the child's parents are examples of some less severe rewards and punishers. While many of these consequences for appropriate or inappropriate behavior are constantly in effect, the teacher will have the best results for extraverted students by reminding them of the rewarding consequences and for introverted students by reminding them of the negative or punishing consequences. Even though exactly the same set of rewarding and punishing consequences actually apply to each student, the teacher can emphasize different consequences as appropriate for different students. It should also be noted that teachers who use either rewards predominantly or punishment predominantly have biased their classrooms in favor of either extraverts or introverts, respectively.

Extraversion and Sex Differences in Achievement

A sex difference in the relationship between extraversion and school achievement has been reported (Naylor, 1972). For elementary school students, extraverted girls have higher achievement scores than introverted girls, while introverted boys have higher achievement than extraverted boys. This sex difference could be a result of different treatment of boys and girls by the predominantly female elementary school teachers. It may also be due to the different effects of peer pressure for boys and girls, if boys' groups tend to reject school and girls' groups tend to accept it more. The extraverted boy, who is highly involved with his peer group, would reject school and perform less well than the less involved introvert, while the extraverted girl's peer group would encourage better school performance.

Summary

The Extraversion-Introversion dimension and its relationship with behavior and learning were described. Extraversion is inversely related to arousal: extraverts usually have lower arousal than introverts. Arousal usually has a curvilinear relationship with performance, so that persons who are moderately aroused perform better than those who are extremely aroused or extremely unaroused. The relationship of arousal and Extraversion with learning and the practical implications for teaching were discussed. Lists of specific recommendations for using Extraversion to individualize instruction are presented in the following chapter.

Readings for "Extraversion-Introversion"

Anthony, W. S. The development of extraversion, of ability, and of the relation between them. *British Journal of Educational Psychology*, 1973, *43*, 223-227.

Anthony, W. S. The development of extraversion and ability: An analysis of Rushton's longitudinal data. *British Journal of Educational Psychology*, 1977, *47*, 193-196.

Brophy, J. E., & Evertson, C. M. *Learning from teaching: A developmental perspective.* Boston: Allyn & Bacon, 1976.

Buss, A. R., & Poley, W. *Individual differences: Traits and factors.* New York: Wiley, 1976.

Entwistle, N. J. Personality and academic attainment. *British Journal of Educational Psychology*, 1972, *42*, 137-151.

Eysenck, H. J. *The biological basis of personality.* Springfield, IL: Thomas, 1967.

Eysenck, H. J. (Ed.). *The measurement of personality.* Baltimore: University Park Press, 1976.

Eysenck, H. J., & Eysenck, S. B. G. *Manual: Eysenck Personality Questionnaire (Junior & Adult).* San Diego: EdITS, 1975.

Eysenck, M. W. Arousal, learning, and memory. *Psychological Bulletin*, 1976, *83*, 389-404.

Gray, J. A. Causal theories of personality and how to test them. In J. R. Royce (Ed.), *Multivariate analysis and psychological theory.* New York: Academic Press, 1973.

Gupta, B. S., & Nagpal, M. Impulsivity/sociability and reinforcement in verbal operant conditioning. *British Journal of Psychology*, 1978, *69*, 203-206.

Honess, T., & Kline, P. Extraversion, neuroticism, and academic attainment in Uganda. *British Journal of Educational Psychology*, 1974, *44*, 74-75.

Naylor, F. D. *Personality and educational achievement.* Sydney: Wiley, 1972.

Wakefield, J. A., Jr., Sasek, J., Brubaker, M. L., & Friedman, A. F. Validity study of the Eysenck Personality Questionnaire. *Psychological Reports*, 1976, *39*, 115-120.

CHAPTER 4: USING EXTRAVERSION – INTROVERSION TO INDIVIDUALIZE INSTRUCTION

Two sets of practical recommendations for individualizing the instruction of extraverted students and introverted students have been drawn from the material presented in the previous chapter. The purpose of these recommendations is to modify the environment and the teacher's behavior to capitalize on the differences in learning styles among these students. Very few of the recommendations deal with changing the child's level of extraversion. Since these practical recommendations follow directly from the material presented in the previous chapter, additional references are not given. Readers who are interested in the research on which the recommendations are based should consult the previous chapter on Extraversion-Introversion and the readings at the end of the chapter. Particular attention should be given to Eysenck (1967), Gray (1973), and Naylor (1972).

Recommendations for Extraverted (high E) Students

1. **Extraverted students should be given short study periods interspersed with different activities.**
    Extraverted students tend to have comparatively short attention spans. They will show momentary lapses of attention when their attention is continually directed toward the same task. If the teacher allows short breaks and changes of activities, the student will work at a task longer and probably will not come to dislike the task as much as under conditions of being forced to continue uninterrupted. The breaks allow these students to work with greater efficiency.

2. **Praise work that is well done.**
    While this is a good procedure with any student, it is particularly effective with extraverted students. Extraverted students are more motivated by signals of reward than by signals of punishment. The teacher's liberal use of praise and constant reminders of rewarding consequences for doing good work will improve the achievement and classroom behavior of these children.

3.   **Direct other students' attention to the extraverted child's good work.**
     The extraverted child likes to be the center of attention. If the attention of other children can be attained by doing school work, more effort may be put into the work. The teacher should, however, carefully note the quality of the other children's reaction to the child's work. If the reaction has negative overtones of, say, derision or jealousy, the teacher should abandon or modify the use of this technique.

4.   **Allow the extraverted child to participate in group work, especially when he can lead the group.**
     The extraverted child prefers to be in the company of others. Such a child should be allowed to work with other children when possible. Group work can be made contingent on good individual work for these children in order to improve the quality of their individual work. For example, a project involving several steps can be assigned to a group. Each child can be required to perform one step (or obtain one piece of information) on his or her own. After each child does an individual task, the group can get together to produce the final product. Allowing the extraverted children to lead occasionally will place them in the center of attention and involve them more thoroughly in the task.

5.   **Use opportunities to work with other children to reward individual work.**
     This recommendation is similar to the one above. However, in cases where the child refuses to do adequate work (work that he or she is capable of) individually, the child can be required to do a small amount of individual work well before being allowed to interact with other children. The length and quality of the required individual assignments can be gradually increased until they are at acceptable levels. Care should be taken that group work not completely replace individual work. Also, the availability of group work should strictly depend on the child's individual work and not be allowed simply because "it is group work time."

6.   **The teacher may have to restrain the extraverted child's impulsive responses by requiring him to "stop and think" before he answers.**
     Although these recommendations are not primarily aimed at changing the child's level of extraversion as such, the characteristic impulsivity of extraverted children requires some control for optimal performance. Extraverted children usually give the first answer to a question that seems "about right." In order to get the correct answer from an extraverted child on the first trial, the teacher may tell the child not to answer until given the instruction "now." If the teacher waits a few seconds between asking the question and saying "now," the child will be allowed to practice improving the answer privately, rather than giving a wrong answer aloud and then correcting it.

7. **After a study period, allow a short break before testing or questioning the extraverted child on the material.**

The extraverted child's performance tends to improve (reminiscence) during a short break without practice immediately following learning new material. The break should be less than 15 minutes long. This period allows the child to consolidate the material learned. Longer breaks, up to half an hour, are not detrimental, but the extraverted child will not have the advantage of reminiscence after these breaks. After even longer delays, these children will be at a disadvantage relative to their introverted classmates.

8. **Use threats of punishment sparingly.**

The extraverted child performs better to obtain rewards than to avoid punishment. Consistent emphasis on punishment for these children will result in punishment being administered frequently without as much effect as could be obtained with the proper use of social rewards. Interestingly, while threats of punishment are not as effective with extraverts as with introverts, the actual administration of punishment is likely to have less serious emotional side effects for extraverts than for introverts. Of course, if the extravert is less responsive to punishment and consequently is punished more often, the emotional reactions can be severe. Using punishment as the predominant disciplinary technique will put extraverted students at a disadvantage relative to introverted students and result in their avoiding school and schoolwork.

Nothing that is said here should be construed as advocating the abandonment of punishment as a disciplinary technique. Recent reviews (see Chapter 9) have shown that (a) punishment is in general more effective for changing behavior than is reward and (b) the emotional side effects of punishment simply do not occur when punishment is used consistently. However, since reward and punishment are differently effective for different students, the teacher should take these individual differences into account in developing disciplinary strategies.

9. **Use stimulating materials with extraverted students.**

Raising the extraverted child's arousal level in any manner should result in improved performance, particularly with easy (for the child) material. Stimulating material will both raise the child's arousal level and direct attention toward the information that is to be learned. Written material can be made stimulating by including colorful pictures and illustrations. The teacher's verbal presentations should be animated and include lively demonstrations. A difficulty arises in that stimulation becomes more important the easier the material is for the child. When it is necessary for the child to "overlearn" basic material, such as addition facts, the material becomes very easy after many repetitions. Nevertheless, overlearning the material will give the child an advantage with later material, and the drill must continue. It is in just such situations that stimulating materials become extremely important.

10. **Games and competition can be used to arouse the extraverted child during schoolwork.**

Another technique for arousing the extraverted child is the use of games and competition in the classroom. Particularly, if the competition is paired with social interaction and encouragement, it will improve the extraverted child's performance. Team competition in spelling and arithmetic will be enjoyable and productive for these children, unless they consistently miss questions and are embarrassed in front of their classmates. The teacher must carefully match the difficulty of questions asked publicly with the child's capabilities. Fortunately, competition is most effective for easy material on which, by definition, the child is more likely to succeed. With very difficult material, lower arousal levels produce better performance and stimulating activities should be avoided.

11. **With extraverted students emphasize broad general principles, rather than details, as much as possible.**

Extraverted students learn those things that are presented strongly. They also forget more information during extended periods of time than their introverted classmates. Constructing quiz items and class questions to emphasize the more strongly presented main points rather than the details will allow these students a greater degree of success. Since they are primarily motivated by rewards, such as success in class, they will be more interested in the material and work harder when general themes are emphasized. Consequently, they should learn more of the details as well.

Of course, details are often so important that they must be emphasized. Where details must be emphasized, they should be presented strongly, repetitiously, and in as stimulating a fashion as possible to extraverted students.

12. **Placing extraverted students under moderate stress may facilitate their performance, especially for easy material.**

Stress is an arouser. Extraverted students generally perform better under moderate stress than under no stress at all. The teacher can create moderate stress by emphasizing the importance of the next test while the child is studying the material. In fact, with extraverted children, a stern lecture about performing well on a test is likely to pay off even when given immediately before a test. Test anxiety is not likely to be a problem with extraverted children unless they are also high on the neuroticism dimension. Using stress to improve the performance of extraverted students will be more effective with easy material than with hard material.

13. **Continuous reinforcement (or feedback) should be given to highly extraverted students.**

Extraverted students should be told how well they are doing as often as possible. Ideally, the material presented to extraverted students would allow them to give correct responses every time and the teacher would then inform them that they were correct after every response. Unfortunately, this degree of individual attention must remain an ideal in a class with one teacher (and possibly an aide) and 25 or more students. However, the teacher should give as much feedback to the extraverted student as is possible, since giving only occasional feedback will place the extraverted student at a disadvantage relative to introverted classmates and result in the student falling behind in schoolwork.

14. **Teachers in the upper grade levels, especially, should concentrate on making their instruction more consistent with the learning styles of extraverted students.**

Although extraverts achieve better than introverts before about age 13 to 14, they fall behind in the higher grades. Teachers in the higher grades can avoid leaving their extraverted students behind by identifying them and applying the other recommendations presented here to those students. These teachers should be careful, however, about modifying their teaching styles generally, since overcompensation in favor of the extraverted students may result in prolonging the early disadvantage of the introverted students.

15. **Boys should be encouraged to act in a less extraverted manner.**

This recommendation is presented with some reluctance, since the sex difference in school achievement—that is, that introverted boys and extraverted girls achieve more—has not been adequately explained. However, a possible explanation is that teachers prefer and/or work more effectively with the more reserved, introverted boys than with the extraverted boys. Since this is a strong possibility, parents, and even teachers themselves, should encourage an extraverted boy to adopt a somewhat more reserved style of behavior at school in order to facilitate his interaction with his teacher.

Recommendations for Introverted (low E) Students

1. **Allow longer periods on a task for introverted students.**

Introverted students maintain their interest in a task longer than their extraverted classmates. They do not like to change tasks as often as extraverts and they profit from longer study periods. The teacher who changes activities for the whole class in response to pressure from the more extraverted students will frustrate the introverts. The shorter times at a task will not allow them to achieve up to their full potential. Further, the introverted students are typically more cautious in their work than the extraverts. During the early part of each period, they will probably work slower than their extraverted classmates. Thus, if the period is ended too soon, the introverted students will have covered less material. However, the introverted students will continue to work productively much longer and should be given the opportunity to do so.

2.   **The teacher should put less emphasis on praising introverted students after doing good work and more emphasis on reassuring them before they begin work.**

Praising the work of introverted students is less effective than praising the work of extraverted students. Introverted students are more motivated to avoid punishment than to obtain praise. While there is no reason for the teacher to avoid praising the introvert's work, it will not be very effective in producing gains in achievement or improved behavior. On the other hand, reassurance prior to taking a test or doing other classwork may be used to lower the introverted student's high level of arousal and thereby improve performance.

3.   **Give feedback to the introverted student in private.**

The introverted student does not like to be the center of attention. Situations in which the introvert becomes the center of attention are unpleasant and are punishing to these students. Since introverted students are primarily motivated to avoid punishment, they will do whatever seems to be necessary to avoid these situations. A well intentioned teacher might try to reward an introverted child for doing good work by calling the attention of the class to such work. This student may learn to do poorer work to avoid what is perceived to be an unpleasant experience.

4.   **Allow the introverted child to work individually as much as possible.**

The introverted child prefers to work alone and does better work individually than in a group. In a group situation, the introverted child will often defer to the other (more extraverted) members of the group. Contributions to the group will be minimal unless the teacher takes steps to enforce participation. The time spent as a peripherally involved group member could be better used working individually.

5.   **Use opportunities to do individual tasks to reward appropriate group participation.**

It is important for the introverted child to learn to participate effectively in groups. To encourage group participation, the teacher can require a certain level of group participation from the introverted child before allowing such children to have time to themselves. At first, the required participation should be minimal, perhaps a single comment. Later the child should be required to participate more substantially before being allowed to work on his or her own. The introverted child will probably continue to prefer individual work, but he will have had opportunities to develop important skills for interacting with others.

6.   **The introverted child may have to be encouraged to be less cautious in responding to questions and giving opinions.**

Typically, the introverted child is cautious. In order to avoid giving an incorrect answer, this child thinks through the response and its implications carefully before responding. Such children may be slow to respond, although they are usually accurate. Often an acceptable response may be judged to be not quite right and will be inhibited in consideration of other possibilities. This slowness to respond can be very frustrating to the teacher, as well as wasteful of time in extreme cases. The introverted child's school performance will improve somewhat if encouraged to be a little less cautious in giving answers and to "say what you think." By avoiding wrong answers at all costs, the child covers less material than might otherwise be covered as well as missing corrective feedback on misconceptions. The teacher can ask the child to say the first thing that comes to his or her mind in response to a question, then allow time to improve an answer before being corrected.

7. **Test or question the introverted child immediately after he studies the material.**
    The introverted child's performance is at its best immediately after having studied the material to be learned. Short breaks between studying and demonstrating competence will work slightly to the disadvantage of these students while longer delays may be to their advantage. Although the amount of information retained continues to decline with time, the decline is less than that of extraverted students. On tests that are remote in time from the original study, such as standardized achievement tests and final exams, the introverted student will have an advantage over the extraverted student, although both will remember less than they knew immediately after studying.

8. **Threats of punishment can be used effectively with introverted students.**
    Care must be exercised in applying this recommendation. While the introverted child will work better to avoid punishment than to obtain a reward, the actual administration of punishment will raise the introvert's (already high) level of arousal, resulting in poorer performance. While the teacher may uniformly apply the same rewards and punishments to all the students, the potential punishments will be more effective for the introverted child. A teacher who uses rewards as the predominant disciplinary technique places introverted children at a disadvantage relative to their extraverted classmates.

9. **Use subdued, "serious-looking" materials with introverted students.**
    The stimulating materials appropriate for extraverted students will over-arouse introverted students except when the material is very easy for the students. In general, the introverted student is fairly highly aroused and additional environmental stimuli arouse him beyond the point of optimal performance. In addition, the introverted student often takes schoolwork seriously and is likely to think of more subdued materials as more important.

10. **Avoid arousing the child during schoolwork.**
    The introverted child is generally highly aroused. For material that is

very easy for such children, they will be at about the optimal arousal level without further environmental stimulation. For difficult material, they may be over-aroused. The teacher's efforts should be directed toward subduing environmental sources of stimulation. Certainly, additional stimulation of the introverted student working on difficult material will be detrimental to performance.

11. **Putting the introverted child under stress to perform well may lower performance, especially with difficult material.**
     Stress to perform well arouses students. Introverted students, who are already fairly highly aroused, do not need additional arousal. Difficult material usually requires a relatively low arousal level for optimal performance. With such material, stress can only be detrimental to the performance of the introverted student. With easy material, stress to perform will probably not lower the introverted student's performance very much. Even with extremely easy material, stress will yield only small improvements in performance for these students.

12. **Details can be emphasized with introverted students.**
     Introverted students learn material that is weakly presented better than extraverted students. Details that are briefly presented in the explanation of a more general point are more likely to be remembered by introverted students. These students can reasonably be tested and questioned on these details without requiring large amounts of class time to be spent on these less important points. Introverted students are successful in learning both details and general points. A teacher who avoids asking detailed questions will not allow the introverted student to demonstrate what has been learned. This may be discouraging and eventually result in less thorough studying.

13. **Encourage the introverted child to initiate interaction.**
     The introverted child prefers not to initiate interactions. However, he or she needs to be able to initiate some interactions. Since introverted children are primarily motivated to avoid punishing situations, the best way to get them to initiate interactions is to assure them that punishment—ridicule or uneasiness—will not follow the initiation of social interaction. They can be given formulas for correct greetings and techniques for opening conversations. Practice in these techniques in a situation that does not make them the center of attention will be helpful. The teacher should be careful that the techniques presented to such students are actually currently acceptable among their peers. For example, formal greetings, such as "good morning, miss," given by one 10-year-old to another will be followed by ridicule, making future social interaction even more difficult for the child.

14. **Teachers at the lower grade levels should concentrate on making their instruction more consistent with the learning styles of introverts.**

Introverted students are at a disadvantage in school until about the age of 13 or 14. Virtually everything that elementary school teachers do in the classroom might as well have been designed to improve the performance of extraverts at the expense of introverts. Short study periods, stimulating material, the growing use of reward techniques to establish and maintain discipline, and the emphasis on general concepts rather than detailed work do not favor introverted students. As these techniques, often labeled progressive, modern, or humanistic, increase in popularity among elementary teachers, we may expect the introverted student's achievement to decline relative to his extraverted classmates. If these techniques come to be widely used in the higher grades, we may see the performance of introverts decline in those grades too. The elementary teacher should identify introverted students and apply the recommendations presented here to those students. However, care must be taken to avoid simply reversing the bias of the classroom to favor introverted students. If all students are subjected to these recommendations for introverted students, the performance of extraverted students may be expected to decline.

15. **Girls should be encouraged to act in a more extraverted manner.**

Extraverted girls and introverted boys achieve more than their other classmates. Although this finding has not been adequately explained, it is likely that extraverted girls are easier for their predominantly female teachers to work with. Introverted girls, but not introverted boys, should be encouraged by their parents and by their teachers to act in a more outgoing manner in the classroom. This may be expected to produce more positive attention from the teacher and better performance on schoolwork.

CHAPTER 5:
NEUROTICISM (EMOTIONALITY)

The following two chapters (5 & 6) deal with Neuroticism (also called emotionality). Chapter 5 contains an overview of the characteristics along this dimension that are relevant to teaching. The interactive characteristics of Neuroticism with Extraversion are also considered. Chapter 6 contains practical recommendations for teaching students who are high (emotional) or low (stable) on this dimension.

Neuroticism, or emotionality, is another widely discussed personality trait. Like extraversion, neuroticism, under a wide variety of names, is a central concept in virtually all theories of personality. Emotionality, emotional problems, poor adjustment, nervousness, and anxiety are all terms which are either roughly equivalent to neuroticism or are a combination of neuroticism and another trait (Eysenck, 1967).

Definition

Neuroticism is the principal dimension of emotional normality-abnormality. Persons on one end of this dimension are thought of as emotionally normal, or even better than normal, and those on the other end are thought of as nervous, maladjusted, or over-emotional. The term "stable" refers to those at one end of the dimension. Neurotic or emotional are terms used for those at the other end. Of course, most people are somewhere between the extremely stable end and the extremely emotional end of the dimension with most people being a little closer to the stable end (Eysenck, 1967).

A person can be very high on the neuroticism dimension and still be moderately well adjusted. While such persons may perform in school adequately and interact reasonably well with family and friends, they will be different in a number of ways from people who are lower on the neuroticism dimension. For instance, they will report that they worry more than others and have a difficult time recovering from emotional experiences.

The abnormal sound of the word "neurotic" should not prejudice the reader against this personality trait. Neurotic simply means nervous. As a mental abnormality it is usually thought of as fairly mild and easily treated. In fact, most neurotics improve in a year or two without any professional help at all (Eysenck, 1973).

It is a good idea to distinguish neurotics from two other groups that are thought of as mentally unsound—psychotics and the mentally retarded. Neurotics are highly emotional people who usually report being unhappy and show adjustment problems. Psychotics are cognitively disordered, showing speech and thought problems and often aggressive behavior problems. Neurotics do not, as a rule, become psychotics. The neuroticism and psychoticism dimensions are independent, as discussed earlier. Mentally retarded persons are those who are low on the intelligence dimension which is also generally unrelated to neuroticism (Eysenck, 1973).

Eysenck describes the person who is high on neuroticism as follows: High N scores are indicative of emotional lability and overreactivity. High scoring individuals tend to be emotionally overresponsive and to have difficulties in returning to a normal state after emotional experiences. Such individuals frequently complain of vague somatic upsets of a minor kind, such as headaches, digestive troubles, insomnia, backaches, etc., and also report many worries, anxieties, and other disagreeable emotional feelings. Such individuals are predisposed to develop neurotic disorders under stress, but such predispositions should not be confused with actual neurotic breakdown; a person may have high scores on N while yet functioning adequately in work, sex, family, and society spheres. (Eysenck & Eysenck, 1975, p.5)

Neuroticism and Behavior

The most characteristic difference between emotional (high neuroticism) and stable (low neuroticism) persons is their reactions to emotional stimuli. Stable persons have very little or no reaction to emotional stimuli. They are very unlikely to become upset and when they do, they recover fairly quickly. Highly emotional persons, on the other hand, react strongly to emotional stimuli, are easily and often upset, and have difficulty returning to a normal low or moderately aroused state. They often adopt various strategies to protect themselves from emotional stimuli such as repressing the material or simply avoiding situations in which emotional encounters are likely to occur (Eysenck, 1967).

Neuroticism and Arousability

A person's neuroticism reflects degree of arousability. A person who is high on neuroticism is more easily aroused than a person lower on this dimension, and is usually in a higher state of arousal. The different arousal levels of these persons are mediated by emotional material. Different arousal levels of people along the neuroticism dimension are distinguished from their different arousal levels along the extraversion dimension in that arousal along the extraversion dimension results from sensory input and problem solving activity rather than from emotional stimuli (Eysenck, 1967).

The relationship between neuroticism and learning in a laboratory situation is similar to, but less pronounced than, the relationship between extraversion and learning (M. Eysenck, 1976). Both personality dimensions are related to the person's arousal level—one emotional arousal and the other cognitive arousal. The relationship is curvilinear: both extremely high and extremely low neuroticism persons typically perform less well than those in the middle. Apparently, the person who is very low on this dimension is not properly motivated to perform well and the person who is high on neuroticism is trying too hard. In fact, neuroticism (sometimes called manifest anxiety) has been used to estimate the subject's level of motivation (or drive) in experiments designed to test basic learning theory (Eysenck, 1967).

External stress interacts with neuroticism in about the same fashion as it interacts with extraversion. External stress applied to a person who is low on neuroticism (low arousal) usually results in improved performance from the subject. In other words, an unmotivated person performs better when given a strong external reason to perform better. External stress applied to a person who is high on neuroticism (high arousal) usually results in poorer performance. That is, the highly motivated person may "try too hard" when given an additional external reason to perform well (Eysenck, 1967).

Test anxiety is often a problem for students who are high on neuroticism. Consistent with the discussion above, when they are told that a test is extremely important or that there are serious consequences for poor performance on a test, they usually are unable to perform well. When they are given the test as a "game" or a rather inconsequential "exercise," they perform much better. Extremely stable students, on the other hand, show little if any debilitating test anxiety. They perform usually better on tests that are presented as being important.

The difficulty of the material being learned is an important consideration. High arousal leads to good performance on very easy material, while lower arousal levels are appropriate for more difficult material. Consequently, the highly aroused (emotional) students usually do well on material that is easy (for them), but not as well as the less aroused (stable) students on more difficult material (Eysenck, 1967).

Neuroticism, Extraversion, and Arousal

The person's levels of extraversion and neuroticism both influence arousal level and thus task performance. The introverted person is more highly aroused than the extraverted person, and the highly neurotic or emotional person is frequently more highly aroused than the stable person. Arousal level is, then, highest for neurotic, introverted (NI) persons and lowest for stable, extraverted (SE) persons. The following figure (5-1) shows the relationship between arousal and performance with the four extreme combinations of extraversion-introversion and neuroticism shown in their approximate positions. The stable introverts (SI) and neurotic extraverts (NE) who have a high arousal trait and a low arousal trait in combination show moderate arousal levels, producing nearly optimal task performance. The other two groups have either extremely high or extremely low arousal and poorer performance (cf. Eysenck, 1976).

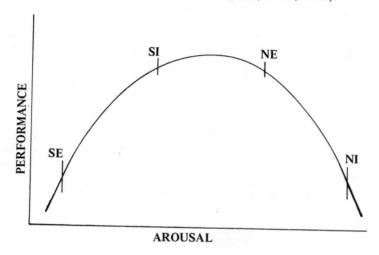

Figure 5-1
Arousal-Performance for Four Personality Combinations

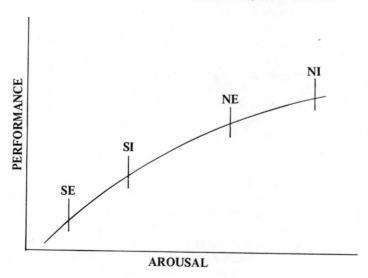

Figure 5-2
Arousal-Performance Relationship for Easy Material

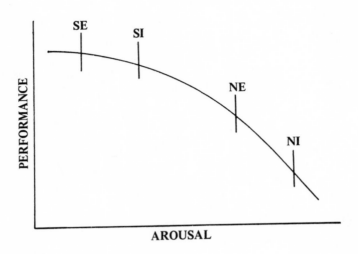

Figure 5-3
Arousal-Performance Relationship for Difficult Material

Both neuroticism and extraversion must be considered in setting the difficulty of the tasks assigned. The first figure (5-1) shows the four extreme groups on a task of intermediate difficulty (for the students, themselves). The relationship between performance and arousal is similar to the second figure (5-2) for very easy material, since higher arousal levels produce better performance for such material. On the other hand, extremely difficult material would produce the third relationship (Fig. 5-3). So, depending on the difficulty of the material, a student with virtually any combination of high or low neuroticism and high or low extraversion can have a marked advantage or a serious disadvantage relative to classmates. By taking this information into account, the teacher may adjust the difficulty of the material when the mismatch between the material and the student is too severe (cf. Eysenck, 1976).

Neuroticism and Achievement

Another characteristic difference between people who are high on neuroticism is the rigidity of their behavior (Eysenck, 1967). Highly emotional persons often have rigid, compulsive behavior, while more stable persons are characterized by freer behavior. One explanation for this difference is that very emotionally arousable persons use rigid, repetitive behavior to protect themselves from coming in contact with emotional stimuli that would over-arouse them. More stable persons do not need to protect themselves from over-arousal and their behavior is more exploratory. In fact, stable students usually perform better under instructions that encourage them to explore, while highly emotional students perform better when the instructor is emotionally supportive, that is, when the instructor helps protect the student from negative emotional stimuli (Trown & Leith, 1975).

The compulsive behavior of the highly emotional student can be, and often is, turned to the student's academic advantage. All that is required is that the repeated behavior be study behavior. Long and frequent study sessions ward off emotional over-arousal and conveniently result in more learning. This may explain why students who are high on neuroticism are often reported to have a slight advantage in academic achievement after about the age of 15. Before that age these students are definitely at a disadvantage relative to their more stable classmates (Entwistle, 1972; Honess & Kline, 1974; Mehryar et al., 1973).

There is no completely satisfactory explanation for this change in relative achievement for stable and emotional students at about age 15. Possibly, the highly emotional students do not learn effective study techniques which, repetitiously applied, work to their advantage, until early in high school. Before that time, their behavior is detrimental to their schoolwork. Another possibility is that the child-oriented elementary teachers simply find stable children more pleasant to work with and inadvertently give the stable children more individual attention and instruction than they give to the more neurotic children. As these students pass from the hands of these teachers to the subject-matter-oriented high school and college teachers, their personality characteristics have less (negative) influence on the teacher. This, combined with more rigid (conscientious) study habits, probably accounts for the highly neurotic student's exchanging early disadvantage for a later advantage in academic work.

The neuroticism and extraversion dimensions yield curiously similar patterns of relationships with academic achievement. For both dimensions, students at the end associated with low arousal (the stable students on the neuroticism dimension and the extraverts on the extraversion dimension) show better academic achievement than their more highly aroused classmates (neurotics and introverts) in the elementary school years and poorer performance in the high school and college years (Entwistle, 1972). Some or all of the differences between elementary school on one hand and high school and college on the other may have different effects on students with different arousal levels (cf., Dunkin & Biddle, 1974). Elementary schools—with child-oriented, mostly female teachers remaining with the students all day, teaching them basic skills individually or in small groups—seem to favor children with lower levels of arousal. High schools and colleges—with subject-oriented, mostly male teachers lecturing for one-hour periods and requiring a substantial amount of work to be done outside class—usually favor students with higher levels of arousal. Adapting characteristics from one level of school to the other may improve the achievement of highly aroused elementary students and less aroused high school and college students.

Neuroticism and Discipline

Gray (1973) has attempted to explain differences in extraversion and neuroticism in terms of sensitivity to signals of reward and punishment. The part of his theory dealing with the extravert's greater sensitivity to reward and the introvert's greater sensitivity to punishment has been discussed earlier. The neuroticism dimension also plays a major role in this theory. Moving along the neuroticism dimension from stable to neurotic, introverts, who are uniformly more sensitive to punishment, become more sensitive to both reward and punishment, but become much more sensitive to punishment. Likewise, extraverts, who are more sensitive to reward, become more sensitive to both reward and punishment than are stable persons. Their relative sensitivity to reward or punishment is determined by their degree of extraversion. Neuroticism amplifies the extravert's sensitivity to reward and the introvert's sensitivity to punishment.

In disciplining students, the teacher will generally be more effective in controlling the behavior of neurotic students than the behavior of stable students regardless of the technique (reward or punishment) used. This means that a teacher who applies exactly the same rewards and punishment to each child in a class will produce some children who are "over-controlled" and some for whom the techniques have little or no effect. Different degrees of reward and punishment must be applied to each child to achieve the same effect. In general, minimal discipline will be effective for highly emotional children, while stable children may require relatively intense discipline.

Particularly, when punishment is used with neurotic introverts, the intensity should be extremely low. In fact, emotional reactions to punishment from these children may be so extreme as to preclude its use with them entirely. Reward should yield satisfactory results with these children. Similarly, reward used with neurotic extraverts may yield reactions that are undesirably strong. For these children, the reward will probably completely distract the child from the task at hand. Punishment may be the only recourse.

On the other hand, reward will probably not have strong enough effects to warrant its use with most stable introverts. Punishment will have correspondingly weak effects with most stable extraverts.

By carefully considering the personality characteristics of the child, the teacher can modify the disciplinary strategy with each one to produce reliable results without producing undue emotional reactions or overcontrolled, inhibited behavior. It should be noted that teachers who make heavy use of any disciplinary measures (rewards or punishment) have biased their classes in favor of stable students. Those who discipline very sparingly or not at all have biased their classes in favor of the highly emotional students.

Summary

The neuroticism dimension and its relationship to behavior and learning were described. Neuroticism indicates emotional arousability: those high on neuroticism are more emotionally arousable than other people. The effects of arousability on learning and behavior, and specifically its interaction with arousal

(Extraversion) on performance, were considered, and practical implications for teaching were discussed. Lists of specific recommendations for using Neuroticism to individualize instruction are presented in the following chapter.

Readings for "Neuroticism"

Bennet, S. N., & Youngman, M. B. Personality and behavior in school. *British Journal of Educational Psychology*, 1973, *43*, 228-233.

Buss, A. R., & Poley, W. *Individual differences: Traits and factors.* New York: Wiley, 1976.

Dunkin, M. J., & Biddle, B. J. *The study of teaching.* New York: Holt, Rinehart & Winston, 1974.

Entwistle, N. J. Personality and academic attainment. *British Journal of Educational Psychology*, 1972, *42*, 137-151.

Entwistle, N. J., & Cunningham, S. Neuroticism and school attainment—a linear relationship. *British Journal of Educational Psychology*, 1968, *38*, 123-132.

Eysenck, H. J. *The biological basis of personality.* Springfield, IL: Thomas, 1967.

Eysenck, H. J. *Handbook of abnormal psychology.* San Diego: EdITS, 1973.

Eysenck, H. J. (Ed.). *The measurement of personality.* Baltimore: University Park Press, 1976.

Eysenck, H. J., & Eysenck, S. B. G. *Manual: Eysenck Personality Questionnaire (Junior & Adult).* San Diego: EdITS, 1975.

Eysenck, M. W. Arousal, learning, and memory. *Psychological Bulletin*, 1976, *83*, 389-404.

Gray, J. A. Causal theories of personality and how to test them. In J. R. Royce (Ed.), *Multivariate analysis and psychological theory.* New York: Academic Press, 1973.

Honess, T., & Kline, P. Extraversion, neuroticism, and academic attainment in Uganda. *British Journal of Educational Psychology*, 1974, *44*, 74-75.

Mehryar, A. H., Khajavi, F., Razavieh, A., & Hosseini, A. Some personality correlates of intelligence and educational attainment in Iran. *British Journal of Educational Psychology*, 1973, *43*, 8-16.

Naylor, F. D. *Personality and educational achievement.* Sydney: Wiley, 1972.

Trown, E. A., & Leith, G. O. M. Decision rules for teaching strategies in primary schools: personality-treatment interactions. *British Journal of Educational Psychology*, 1975, *45*, 130-140.

CHAPTER 6: USING NEUROTICISM TO INDIVIDUALIZE INSTRUCTION

Two sets of practical recommendations for individualizing the instruction of students at the extremes of the neuroticism dimension will be presented. The first set is for students who are high on neuroticism. The second set is for students who are low or about average on neuroticism. All the recommendations in the second set apply, as written, to the student who is average on neuroticism and, in stronger form, to the student who is extremely low on neuroticism.

These recommendations are designed to take advantage of individual differences in neuroticism to enhance academic achievement and classroom behavior. Few of the recommendations deal with changing the student's neuroticism directly, although in extreme cases, efforts toward this end might be appropriate. For most students, it is far more efficient to take their levels of neuroticism into account during teaching than to try to change their personalities to fit the teaching. If we tried to change their levels of neuroticism to improve their performance, we would have to do so several times, since, as previously discussed, different levels of neuroticism are most advantageous for school achievement at different ages.

Readers who are interested in the research on which these recommendations are based should consult the previous chapter on Neuroticism and the readings at the end of the chapter. Particular attention should be given to Eysenck (1967), Gray (1973), and Naylor (1972).

Recommendations for Students Who Are High on Neuroticism (Emotional)

1. **Praise the work that the neurotic student does well.**

    Highly neurotic students are very sensitive to both praise and punishment. Praise from the teacher will usually result in increased achievement or, when the student is already performing well, it will maintain the achievement. Praise will also reassure the child and should gradually reduce anxiety concerning school and academic work. A note of caution is necessary in using praise or any other reward with children who are high on both neuroticism and extraversion. These children are so sensitive to rewards that the rewards may distract them from the task at hand. If the teacher sees that the child's attention is focused on the reward to the exclusion of the task, rewards should be discontinued.

2. **The threat of punishment is effective for neurotic children, but actual punishment may be detrimental to their performance.**

    Neurotic students are sensitive to signals of punishment, as well as praise. Threatening punishment can be used as an effective technique for changing or maintaining the behavior of these children. Special caution should be exercised when using threats of punishment with students who are high on neuroticism and extremely low on extraversion (neurotic introverts). These students are so sensitive to threats of punishment that such threats may inhibit a good deal of desirable behavior along with the undesirable. These students appear over-controlled. Their extreme efforts to avoid punishment may inhibit even the slightest exploration of the material, since exploration can lead to wrong, and to these children, "punishable" answers.

    The teacher should also try to avoid actually having to administer punishment to these children. They are slow to recover from emotional experiences. Their heightened emotional arousal after punishment will interfere with their learning for a fairly long period. Also, the punishment can be expected to increase their fears about school and result in lessened achievement in the long run.

3. **Avoid emotional experiences, especially negative ones, with these children.**

    Highly neurotic children are easily aroused by emotional situations. The resultant arousal level will usually be too high to allow optimal performance at schoolwork. In addition, their recovery from emotional arousal is slow. The usual result of emotional experiences for neurotic children is to lower their performance and to keep it low for a much longer period of time than the teacher would expect. While this is true of both pleasant and unpleasant emotional experiences, the unpleasant ones may increase the child's fears of school as well as over-arousing him.

4. **Avoid stress to perform well, especially with difficult (for the child) material.**

    The child who is high on the neuroticism dimension is easily aroused by environmental stress. If the teacher puts pressure on the child to perform well, the child will probably be too highly aroused to do so. Extremely high arousal is particularly detrimental to performance on difficult material. To perform well on difficult material, the child should be as relaxed as possible. Higher levels of arousal are not as detrimental to, and may enhance, the child's performance on very easy material. When deciding how much pressure is appropriate, the teacher should consider the relationship between arousal and difficulty of the material. Also, she should consider difficulty in relation to the child and not think of it as absolute difficulty. For instance, although division may be absolutely more difficult than addition, addition should be considered difficult for a child who has not been previously exposed to it, while division may be easy for a child with a considerable amount of practice with it.

5.   **Use relaxation techniques and desensitization to specific fears.**

This recommendation is best applied by, or under the supervision of, a trained psychologist. The highly neurotic child is much more likely to have specific fears concerning various aspects of school than other children are. These fears can be reduced by presenting the feared stimulus to the child at reduced intensity and gradually increasing the intensity to the level at which the child experiences the stimulus at school. The initial presentation may use a picture rather than the feared object itself. At each step in this process, the child is instructed to relax in the presence of the object (or its representation). Gradually, the child should become able to tolerate the feared object, and eventually he should lose his fear completely. It is important that a psychologist direct this treatment, since its incorrect application may increase the child's fear.

6.   **Discourage either extreme impulsivity or extreme caution, but do not allow the child to go to the opposite extreme.**

For the highly neurotic child, either extremely impulsive or extremely cautious behavior is likely depending on the child's level of extraversion. If the child is also high on extraversion, impulsivity is to be expected; if low on extraversion (introverted), cautious, inhibited behavior is likely. Both extremes are detrimental to learning. The impulsive child answers incorrectly too often, resulting in discouragement. The overly cautious child does not take necessary chances to test the grasp of material that has not been completely learned. An intermediate style, combining moderate reflection and a willingness to make reasonable guesses after considering the material, is the most advantageous for school achievement. Since the highly neurotic child's behavior is easily influenced by the teacher's actions, care must be taken that behavior is not simply pushed from one extreme to the other. When the teacher strongly encourages the neurotic child to do the opposite of what the child has been doing, over-compensation is very likely.

7.   **A subdued, personal approach is called for with neurotic children.**

Highly neurotic children are easily aroused emotionally. Their over-arousal is usually detrimental to their schoolwork. The teacher will get as much response from these children by speaking softly and behaving in a reserved manner as would result from loud, animated behavior with other children. Avoiding this kind of behavior with highly neurotic children will reduce the chance of their becoming too aroused to do their work.

8. **De-emphasize testing and evaluation of work for highly neurotic children.**
Students who are high on the neuroticism dimension suffer more from test anxiety and its detrimental effects than do other children. The teacher can reduce test anxiety by de-emphasizing the importance of classroom tests. The teacher can refer to them as exercises rather than tests and give the child some flexibility concerning when the test is taken. The test can then be taken when the child is relatively calm and confident. Ideally, tests would be avoided altogether with these children. Their achievement could be rated by sampling from assignments completed under minimal stress. Of course, these children must learn to study for and take tests and cope with the attendant anxiety. Tests cannot, then, be entirely avoided, but they can be administered in as relaxed a manner as possible.

9. **Give frequent tests rather than a single final.**
Highly emotional children perform better on frequent tests than on a single final exam. In fact, they are at a considerable disadvantage on a single, extremely important test. The reason for this is probably that the emotional students experience the greater stress associated with more important tests more strongly than their classmates. Their performance on the test is lower than on other work, while some of their less emotional classmates will perform better than usual due to the stress. Frequent, less critical, tests arouse less anxiety and allow emotional students to perform much better.

10. **Avoid arousing the emotional child during his work.**
Allow these children to work quietly as much as possible. While the teacher will have to present work in an animated, excited fashion to motivate some students, this approach is detrimental to the performance of emotional students who are likely to react too strongly.

11. **Structure the child's time and environment as much as possible.**
Making the child's school day very predictable will reduce anxiety and allow better performance. If "surprises" happen too often at school, the emotional child will stay on edge trying to anticipate them. This is true whether the surprises are pleasant or unpleasant. Both will often excite the child beyond the point where he or she can perform adequately.
Particular mention should be made of using ordered turns for oral responses with emotional children. Ordered turns, or letting the children know well ahead of time when they will be called on, is generally superior to random turns with younger children. With emotional children, it has the added advantage of avoiding surprises and allowing the child to recover from anxiety between turns. Maintaining high arousal by making the turns unpredictable is detrimental for these children.

12.   **When the emotional child is upset, allow him to postpone his work until another time.**

When a child is upset performance may be below that child's normal performance. Emotional children are upset more often than their classmates. Being required to work while upset will not only result in lower performance on that particular piece of work but will associate working and being upset and thus lower performance on future work. In applying this recommendation, the teacher must be careful not to let the child use being upset to manipulate the amount of work he is required to do. If the teacher sees that applying this recommendation reduces the total amount of work the child does over, say, a week, she should be somewhat more rigid about when work is done. It is better to implement or discontinue this recommendation gradually. Sudden implementation will encourage the child to manipulate the teacher, and sudden discontinuation will be frustrating for the child.

13.   **The teacher should give the highly neurotic child a good deal of emotional support.**

Reassurance that they are performing adequately is even more important for highly emotional children than it is for others. The emotional support reduces anxiety, allowing improved performance, which then allows praise and credible encouragement. The teacher should, however, be careful not to be more supportive after failure than after success. Although support may seem more necessary after failure, additional attention at that point can result in the child's failing in order to get the attention. The teacher should be particularly supportive when the child is doing adequate work in order to avoid the negative effects of attention given at the wrong time.

14.   **Elementary teachers, especially, should identify highly neurotic children and modify their teaching for them.**

Neurotic students are at a disadvantage to their less emotional classmates in elementary school achievement. While the exact reason for this is unclear, recommendations have been given to improve the performance of students who are high on neuroticism. By identifying the highly emotional children in the class, the teacher can apply these recommendations to specific children and compensate for their usual disadvantage in the elementary grades. Of course, the recommendations should be applied only to the appropriate students. If the teacher simply applies these recommendations to the class in general, it may create a disadvantageous situation for the less neurotic students, rather than allowing all the students to perform optimally.

Recommendations for Students with Low or Average Levels of Neuroticism (Stable)

1.   **Praise and punishment must be intense to achieve results with children who are low on neuroticism.**

Children who are low on neuroticism are relatively insensitive to both praise and punishment: the lower the child is on this dimension, the more difficult it will be to influence behavior by any technique. When considering appropriate disciplinary techniques for a stable child, it is necessary to consider the level of extraversion. Although relatively insensitive to disciplinary techniques, stable extraverts are more susceptible to reward than to punishment and stable introverts are more susceptible to punishment than to reward. In most cases, the teacher will be able to influence the stable child's behavior adequately by selecting the technique to which that child is more susceptible and applying that technique somewhat more intensely than would be necessary with a more emotional child. This recommendation is particularly important for students with extremely low levels of neuroticism.

2. **Stress to perform well should enhance the performance of stable students, especially with easy material.**
    Students who are low on neuroticism frequently show little motivation to perform well on schoolwork. Unlike their more emotional classmates, external stress usually facilitates their performance. Also, these students are unlikely to show negative emotional effects from being subjected to stress by the teacher. Particularly when stable students are working with material that is very easy for them, they will require external stress as a source of motivation and the teacher should be willing to supply it. Two situations will arise with these students when the teacher should be careful not to apply too much stress. First, difficult (for the child) material requires lower levels of arousal for best performance; thus, less external stress is called for. Second, stable children with low levels of extraversion (introverts) are more aroused than other stable children and require less, if any, external stress to perform optimally.

3. **Strong emotional experiences may be motivating for stable children.**
    While it was suggested that the teacher avoid emotional experiences with neurotic children who are likely to over-react, strong emotional experiences have only a moderately arousing effect on stable children. This smaller effect will usually facilitate the child's school performance. For this reason, administering very stimulating rewards and punishment need not be avoided as they often must be with more emotional students. Generally, rewards will not distract the stable student from the task at hand, and punishment will not have undesirable side effects. A teacher who avoids these two techniques entirely will simply favor the emotional students.

4. **Use stimulating material with stable students.**
    The material used with stable students should be emotionally stimulating. Stories to be read should have as much excitement in them as possible. Material with a neutral emotional tone, such as descriptions or rational arguments often will not interest these students unless the teacher strongly

emphasizes how such material may be related to exciting or adventurous topics. A teacher with a large number of stimulating applications of school material, and who shows personal enthusiasm for the material, will be most effective with stable students. The teacher should not forget, however, that this stimulation is unnecessary and may even be detrimental for the more emotional students in the class.

5.   **Emphasize the importance of tests and evaluation of classwork.**
     Stable students are not usually subject to test anxiety as are their more emotional classmates. Being reminded that they are being evaluated, that poor performance will disappoint the teacher and possibly lead to unpleasant consequences, and that good performance will please the teacher and possibly lead to desirable consequences, generally will result in improved performance for stable students. Further, giving a smaller number of tests emphasizes the importance of each test and, thus, facilitates the performance of stable students. The teacher is faced with a serious problem in that emphasizing the importance of tests results in poorer performance for the more emotional children. The different needs of both groups require that the teacher have frequent individual discussions with the students about tests and classwork and give individual feedback after tests. During these discussions, the teacher can tailor the emphasis to the child's level of emotionality in order to allow optimal performance from each one.

6.   **Encourage stable children to explore material, and allow them to discover information on their own.**
     Allowing stable students some independence in dealing with school material allows them to achieve at a higher level than when they are carefully directed. Especially, encouraging active exploration allows stable children to focus on parts of the material that are particularly interesting to them. The stimulation obtained from these parts may increase performance on less interesting material. Stable students have a preference for directing their own learning and work more enthusiastically when allowed to do so. In applying this recommendation, the teacher should not forget that encouraging independence will often be detrimental for more highly emotional students. Once again, different students learn optimally under different conditions.

7.   **High school and college teachers, in particular, should identify students with extremely low levels of neuroticism and modify their treatment of them.**
     Students with extremely low levels of neuroticism are usually found to be at a disadvantage to their more neurotic classmates in high school and college. The disadvantage is especially pronounced at the college level. Perhaps the more structured coursework, or less personal involvement with the teacher, or the lower interest in discipline among these teachers result in a disadvantage for the less emotional students. Performance in these years is more

dependent on individual motivation, which is usually higher for the more emotional students, than on encouragement and attention from the teacher. Stable students, and especially those with extremely low neuroticism, may work better under an individual tutor who can pay more attention to motivating that one student, than in a large impersonal class. Of course, a high school or college teacher who drastically changes the entire teaching procedure in favor of more personal attention, more stimulation, and more discipline will simply put the more emotional students at a disadvantage. Changes in procedure must be directed at individual students, not at entire classes.

CHAPTER 7:
PSYCHOTICISM (TOUGH–MINDEDNESS)

The following two chapters (7 & 8) deal with Psychoticism (also called tough-mindedness). Chapter 7 contains an overview of the characteristics along this dimension that are relevant to teaching. The interactive characteristics of Psychoticism with the other two personality dimensions are also discussed. Chapter 8 contains practical recommendations for teaching students who are high or low on this dimension.

Psychoticism, or tough-mindedness, is a second personality dimension associated with abnormality. The low end of the dimension is associated with persons who are very unlikely to have "psychotic" breaks and whose behavior and cognitive styles are very disimilar to psychotics. The high end of the dimension is associated with behavior and cognitive styles similar to those seen in clinical psychotic populations (Eysenck & Eysenck, 1976; Friedman et al., 1976).

Definition

Although a person can have a very high level of psychoticism and still function adequately, stress or other environmental factors are more likely to result in a display of psychotic behavior for these people than for those who are lower on this dimension. Psychoticism does not completely determine who will actually become psychotic. One person with a very high level and fortunate enough to live in a very unstressful environment may not have a psychotic break, although the same person might in a different environment. Similarly, someone with a lower level of psychoticism in a harsher environment might become psychotic. Those with extremely low levels of psychoticism are very unlikely to display psychotic behavior in any environment (Eysenck & Eysenck, 1976).

Since environment and psychoticism must both be involved to produce a psychotic, we can see a wide variation in psychoticism among normal persons (Eysenck & Eysenck, 1976). For this reason, it is important to point out that high levels of psychoticism are not necessarily "abnormal," although the behavior of persons with high psychoticism is in many respects similar to psychotics. In order to avoid implying that persons who are high on psychoticism are abnormal, the term "tough-minded" is often substituted. The opposite term "tender-minded" refers to those with low levels of psychoticism. Almost all people are somewhere between these two extremes with most people being a little closer to the tender-minded end of the dimension.

Eysenck describes the tough-minded, or high psychoticism person as: . . . solitary, not caring for people; he is often troublesome, not fitting in anywhere. He may be cruel and inhumane, lacking in feeling and empathy, and altogether insensitive. He is hostile to others, even his own kith and kin, and aggressive, even to loved ones. He has a liking for odd and unusual things and a disregard for danger; he likes to make fools of other people and to upset them. This is a description of adult high P scores; as far as children are concerned, we obtain a fairly congruent picture of an odd, isolated troublesome child; glacial and lacking in human feelings for his fellow-beings and for animals; aggressive and hostile, even to near-and-dear ones. Such children try to make up for lack of feeling by indulging in sensation-seeking "arousal jags" without thinking of the dangers involved. Socialization is a concept which is relatively alien to both adults and children; empathy, feelings of guilt, sensitivity to other people are notions which are strange and unfamiliar to them. This description, of course, refers in its entirety only to extreme examples; persons perhaps scoring relatively high, but nearer the middle range of scores, would of course be far more frequent than extremes, and would only show these behavior patterns to a much less highly developed degree. Psychiatric terms which would seem to assimilate this kind of behavior pattern are "schizoid" and "psychopathic"; "behavior disorders" is another term which springs to mind. Our concept of "psychoticism" overlaps with all three of these diagnostic terms. (Eysenck & Eysenck, 1975, pp. 5-6).

Tender-minded persons (low psychoticism) are exactly the opposite of this description. They may be described as empathic, sensitive, and not aggressive or hostile. They are well socialized and have few, if any, problem behaviors.

Psychoticism and Behavior Problems

The psychoticism dimension is highly related to the occurrence of behavior problems in school children (Saklofske, 1977). Those who are high on this dimension have many problem behaviors, while those who are low on this dimension seldom show problem behaviors. Persons who are high on psychoticism are considered more immature and irresponsible than others. They also are opposed to authority and difficult to handle. Neither their peers nor authority figures seem to be able to control the behavior of children who are high on psychoticism as well as they control the behavior of others. Vandalism, stealing, violence, breaking and entering, and serious school misbehavior are all associated with high psychoticism, but not with the other two dimensions

(Eysenck & Eysenck, 1976).

Psychoticism should be clearly distinguished from neuroticism. Psychoticism is associated with aggressive behavior and cognitive defects; neuroticism is associated with emotional instability and nervousness. The two dimensions are unrelated to each other. It is possible for a person to be high on neuroticism and low on psychoticism—a nervous and sensitive, unaggressive person. Another person might be low on neuroticism and high on psychoticism—a calm, emotionally stable and cold, aggressive person. It is just as likely that a person could be low on both—an emotionally stable, unaggressive person—or high on both—an emotionally unstable, aggressive person (Eysenck & Eysenck, 1969).

This is consistent with research on children's behavior in school. Although a wide variety of names have been used, two major syndromes in school children have been repeatedly discovered and discussed. These are often referred to as "emotional problems" and "behavior problems" (Kohn, 1977). These two syndromes usually occur in different children and present different problems to teachers and psychologists who work with them. A child with emotional problems, like our highly emotional (neurotic) child is anxious, fearful, and easily upset but does not usually disrupt the class. A child with behavior problems, on the other hand, disrupts class and attacks other children, but shows little or no anxiety or even fear of punishment. The independent neuroticism and psychoticism dimensions, then, correspond to distinct emotional and behavioral problem syndromes, respectively.

Psychoticism and Arousal-Seeking

Another distinction between psychoticism and neuroticism has to do with arousal. The neuroticism dimension indicates emotional arousal, with highly neurotic persons being highly aroused and easy to arouse even further. Psychoticism seems not to be directly related to arousal. Persons with high levels of psychoticism are no more or less aroused than others. People with high psychoticism do, however, seek environmental stimulation. They do dangerous or exciting things without considering the consequences, apparently simply to increase their arousal. This type of activity is not characteristic of persons with lower levels of psychoticism. While psychoticism is not related to differences in arousal, it is related to differences in how gratifying high arousal states are (Eysenck & Eysenck, 1976).

Practically, it is important to recognize that persons with high psychoticism will seek out ways to arouse themselves, regardless of whether the ways seem pleasant or unpleasant to others. This person may provoke punishment or outbursts from authority figures simply for the stimulation. Vigorous punishment will often increase, rather than inhibit, misbehavior for these persons, as will loud, emotional displays.

The relationship between the three personality dimensions and arousal may be summarized in three statements. Extraversion reflects basic differences in arousal itself, with introverts being more highly aroused than extraverts. Neuroticism reflects differences in arousability, with highly neurotic persons being easier to arouse and consequently usually in a relatively high state of arousal. Psychoticism reflects differences in *seeking* high arousal, with highly psychotic persons seeking high arousal.

The tendency of people who are high on psychoticism to seek out arousing situations probably explains, at least partially, many of their other characteristics. Aggressive and irresponsible acts are often followed by arousing situations. Opposing authority figures allows continual stimulation with very little effort (Eysenck & Eysenck, 1976).

Tough-minded persons are also often impulsive (Eysenck & Eysenck, 1976). Their tendency to respond quickly without much thought, of course, often results in mistakes with stimulating consequences. Since this is what the highly psychotic person is seeking, the consequences do not inhibit future thoughtless behavior. In fact, negative (to most of us) consequences may have a slight tendency to make the behavior more probable in the future.

Psychoticism and Learning

Highly psychotic persons have been reported not to learn from experience as as well as others (Eysenck & Eysenck, 1976). While most people learn not to do harmful things after being hurt only once, these people repeat the harmful behavior again and again, seeming not to remember the harmful effects. A better explanation for this pattern of behavior is that the arousing effects outweigh the physical harm, resulting in continued harmful behavior. Consistent with their not learning well from experience, highly psychotic persons seem not to benefit from therapy as much as others. They are more likely to fail to follow instructions and to drop out of therapy. They make slower progress, and when left in therapy until their behavior improves substantially, they take longer than others (Eysenck & Eysenck, 1976).

Persons with high levels of psychoticism often score high on tests of creativity or originality. This is consistent with the wide-spread view that creativity and psychotic disorders share a common element. Persons with moderately high levels of psychoticism make more unusual associations than do those with lower levels. Some of these unusual associations are interesting or productive and are judged to be creative. When this tendency to make unusual associations goes too far, it is judged to be bizarre or disorganized as in psychotic fantasies (Woody & Claridge, 1977).

The effects of these persons' unusual associations is probably influenced by their intelligence. Since intelligence and psychoticism are unassociated (or at most, there is a very slight negative relationship), it is possible to find some highly psychotic persons who are very intelligent and some who are very dull. It has been suggested that intelligence makes the difference between creative persons and psychopaths. Intelligent persons high on psychoticism are able to use their unusual thought processes toward productive ends. Unintelligent, highly psychotic persons can neither cope with nor make themselves understood by others. They are often institutionalized to prevent destructive behavior (Eysenck & Eysenck, 1976).

Psychoticism and Achievement

While there is very little if any association between psychoticism and intelligence, there is definitely a strong negative relationship between psychoticism and achievement (Eysenck & Eysenck, 1976). The person with a high level of psychoticism does not perform as well in courses as do students with lower levels of psychoticism at any educational level from elementary school to adult courses. The strong and consistent relationship between psychoticism and school achievement and its independence of intelligence make it imperative to consider this personality dimension in planning any instructional program. Unlike extraversion and neuroticism which influence achievement oppositely at different educational levels, psychoticism has a consistent influence on achievement throughout school. Psychoticism is, then, similar to intelligence in that it will identify students who will be consistently advantaged or disadvantaged in school.

Explanations for the consistent disadvantage of students with high levels of psychoticism are not hard to construct. The behavior problems of these students force teachers to spend more time and energy constructing disciplinary strategies than instructional strategies for these students. Since the disciplinary strategies are not usually very effective with these students, their teachers often try to get them out of their classes (cf. Kohn, 1977).

Even in the absence of disruptive behavior, their tendency toward unusual associations may convince the teacher that they either are not paying attention or are not able to understand what is being taught. Even the student whose high psychoticism is offset by high intelligence, may not be considered one of the teacher's more enjoyable students, although that student's originality may be recognized.

In addition to behavior problems and unusual associations, students with high levels of psychoticism have difficulty maintaining their attention on a single task for long periods of time. Studies considering muscle potential while attending to a task indicate that concentration requires more effort from high psychotic persons than from persons low on psychoticism. Increased effort was not related to extraversion or neuroticism. Problems in maintaining attention can also contribute to the academic problems of the student with a high level of psychoticism (Eysenck & Eysenck, 1976).

Psychoticism and Sex

There is a sex difference in psychoticism with males on the average being at higher levels than females (Eysenck & Eysenck, 1976). This difference is consistent with the much higher incidence of behavior problems and aggressive acts among boys than among girls, and the higher incidence of psychotic disorders among males than among females. This difference also parallels the difference in academic achievement between the sexes. Although there is no sex difference in general intelligence, girls as a group receive higher grades than boys. Also, at any grade level, a girl will probably have a higher grade average than a boy with exactly the same measured intelligence. Although high levels of psychoticism are more frequent among boys, high psychoticism is also associated with anti-social behavior and low achievement among girls.

Psychoticism and Other Dimensions

The effects of high psychoticism are moderated by other variables. The effect of intelligence in distinguishing between creatives and psychopaths among those high in psychoticism has been mentioned. It is also possible for persons high on psychoticism to be either high or low on neuroticism. Neuroticism, here, seems to distinguish between those who capably execute anti-social acts (low neuroticism) and those who ineffectively attempt such acts (high neuroticism). Also, extraversion affects the actions of persons high on psychoticism. For anti-social and criminal behavior, extraverts are more likely to direct their acts against people (violence), while introverts are more likely to direct their acts at inanimate objects (property crimes). When psychotic breaks occur, extraverts become manic, and introverts become schizophrenic (Eysenck & Eysenck, 1976).

Summary

The Psychoticism dimension and its relationship with behavior and learning were described. Psychoticism indicated arousal-seeking and its concomitant behavior problems and unusual responses: those high on psychoticism seek arousing stimuli more, show more behavior problems, and give more unusual responses than other people. The effects of these characteristics on learning and behavior were considered, and practical implications for teaching were discussed. Lists of specific recommendations for using Psychoticism to individualize instruction are presented in the following chapter.

Readings for "Psychoticism"

Bandura, A., & Walters, R. *Social learning and personality development.* New York: Holt, Rinehart & Winston, 1963.

Eysenck, H. J. (Ed). *The measurement of personality.* Baltimore: University Park Press, 1976.

Eysenck, H. J., & Eysenck, S. B. G. *Manual: Eysenck Personality Questionnaire (Junior & Adult).* San Diego: EdITS, 1975.

Eysenck, H. J., & Eysenck, S. B. G. *Psychoticism as a dimension of personality.* London: Hodder & Stoughton, 1976.

Eysenck, S. B. G., & Eysenck, H. J. 'Psychoticism' in children: A new personality variable. *Research in Education,* 1969, *1,* 21-37.

Friedman, A. F., Wakefield, J. A., Jr., Boblitt, W. E., & Surman, G. Validity of psychoticism scale of the Eysenck Personality Questionnaire. *Psychological Reports,* 1976, *39,* 1309-1310.

Kohn, M. *Social competence, symptoms and underachievement in childhood: A longitudinal perspective.* New York: Wiley, 1977.

Saklofske, D. H. Personality and behavior problems of schoolboys. *Psychological Reports,* 1977, *41,* 445-446.

Woody, E., & Claridge, G. Psychoticism and thinking. *British Journal of Social and Clinical Psychology,* 1977, *16,* 241-248.

CHAPTER 8: USING PSYCHOTICISM TO INDIVIDUALIZE INSTRUCTION

Two sets of practical recommendations for individualizing instruction will be presented for the psychoticism dimension. The first set applies to students with high levels of psychoticism. Since students who are low on this dimension seem not to be at a disadvantage in any educational setting, few special recommendations are made for them.

The recommendations made for the students with high levels of psychoticism may be applied in moderation with any students whose psychoticism levels are above average. For students with average or low levels of psychoticism, it is best to plan their treatment using the other dimensions, primarily, and to consider the recommendations for low psychoticism as secondary in importance.

As with the recommendations for the other dimensions, the primary goal of these is to use the characteristics of individuals to enhance their learning, rather than to change their characteristics. Since students with high levels of psychoticism are always at a disadvantage, it might seem appropriate to focus on lowering the psychoticism of these students, and with extremely high levels there may be no reasonable alternative. However, two considerations suggest that the focus of treatment not be on changing their psychoticism but on adapting teaching techniques to their characteristics and using these characteristics, as much as possible, to the students' advantage. First, persons with high levels of psychoticism have simply not been as responsive to therapy as have others. Second, if creativity is substantially a combination of high intelligence and high psychoticism (or at least the unusual associates part of it) (cf. Woody & Claridge, 1977), lowering psychoticism can be considered equivalent to stifling creativity. The second consideration, of course, does not apply to those with lower intelligence.

Readers who are interested in the original research on which these recommendations are based should consult the previous chapter on Psychoticism and the readings at the end of the chapter. Eysenck and Eysenck (1976) is the central work on this personality dimension.

Recommendations for Students Who Are High on Psychoticism (Tough-Minded)

1. **Stimulating punishment should be avoided whenever possible.**

   The student who is high on psychoticism often seeks arousing situations regardless of the pain associated with them. In fact, the pain may be part of the stimulation sought. Physical punishment and loud, emotional reprimands will increase the frequency of the undesirable behavior, rather than inhibit it, for these students. Another reason to avoid physical punishment with these students is that they may copy the aggression against them and become more likely to use this stimulating technique against others (cf. Bandura & Walters, 1963). Effective punishment of these children consists of depriving them of an arousing situation following misbehavior. Spending time in enforced inactivity in a quiet, uninteresting room following misbehavior should inhibit the misbehavior. Of course, if the teacher engages in an emotional (stimulating) lecture or argument with the student, the effect will be completely lost. While physical restraint may be necessary to stop a behavior (particularly a harmful one) while the child is engaged in it, physical punishment may not effectively eliminate the behavior.

2. **Use loud, stimulating activities to encourage appropriate behavior.**

   The tough-minded student should be allowed to find appropriate stimulation through appropriate behavior. While it is unlikely that the teacher can make teaching as arousing as the student can (make the environment), some stimulation can be allowed by giving the student bright, interesting materials and allowing play activities only after a period of appropriate behavior.

3. **Allow the child to participate in competitive activity following studying or other quiet activity.**

   The student with a high level of psychoticism will work to be allowed to participate in competitive activity. The teacher who allows the child to participate in competition only in response to studying presents a way for the child to seek arousal through quiet work. The study periods must be short for the child to understand the connection.

4. **Channel competitiveness into schoolwork.**

   Although extreme competition is disturbing to some children, tough-minded students usually like competition. While they probably would not participate enthusiastically in a spelling exercise, a spelling contest may be exciting. Of course, the teacher who uses competition to provoke participation from a student with a high level of psychoticism must keep several things in mind as it is used. First, the best interests of other students should not be sacrificed in meeting the needs of one student. If other students react negatively to competition or if they feel that they lose often or that the competition is at their expense, it should be discontinued. Second, competition will not motivate the student with high psychoticism unless it is actually exciting. The student who consistently either wins or loses may lose interest.

5. **Allow the student with high psychoticism to work for short periods with frequent breaks.**

These students have to work harder at maintaining their attention on a task than other students do. The teacher should not attempt to hold the child's attention for too long. Long attention demands may provide an opportunity for a hostile outburst which will probably be arousing and encourage further outbursts. The length of the study periods can be gradually increased, but increasing them too suddenly can be expected to lead to disruption.

6. **Have the child plan activities ahead of time and follow those plans in an orderly manner.**

Students with high levels of psychoticism seldom make plans and are easily distracted from their plans when they do have them. The teacher should ask the child to list (or say) the things to be done during a short study period. The student can then check items off the list as they are done. The teacher can allow the student to take a break or engage in another activity when the last item is checked. The teacher will have to monitor the child to assure that he or she is not distracted from the list, especially at first.

7. **The teacher may have to remind the child with high psychoticism about the overall goal occasionally during work.**

Students with high psychoticism have difficulty staying with the point. When talking, they often forget their main point and follow a side issue that momentarily attracts their attention. Similarly, when working alone, they often get slightly off task. The teacher should monitor assigned work closely and be ready to reorient these students to the overall goal of their work. At other times, the teacher should encourage these children to follow their own impulses even though what is produced may seem disorganized.

8. **Encourage the student to stop and think before responding.**

Children with high levels of psychoticism are usually impulsive. When asked a question, they respond quickly at the expense of accuracy. Their impulsivity is related to their tendency to get off the topic when they talk and to produce unusual associations. Other children are better at inhibiting their deviations from the topic in order to make their point, although all children have some trouble staying on the topic. The teacher should require the child to wait a short period, say one or two seconds, before answering a question when he or she seems to be answering without thinking.

9. **Material rewards may influence the tough-minded child's behavior more than social rewards.**

For most children, social rewards, such as praise from the teacher, attention from other children, and approval from parents, are more effective for producing acceptable behavior and learning than are material rewards, such as candy or toys. The child with high psychoticism often will be unresponsive to social rewards. Although material rewards will also be only minimally effective with these children, they may prove to be more effective than social rewards. The teacher who attempts to use material rewards for the benefit of a highly psychotic student should be aware of two problems to be faced. First, if material rewards are used for only one (or a few) children, the other children may think the teacher is being unfair. Second, if material rewards are used for the entire class, most of the children will not benefit from the practice, although they will like it. In fact, when social rewards are replaced with material, the achievement and discipline of most students can be expected to decline. A solution to this dilemma is to have someone outside the class—a counselor, principal, or parent—administer the material rewards to the student upon the teacher's recommendation.

10.   **Allow the child to work on creative projects as much as possible.**
    Children with high levels of psychoticism produce unusual associations, and when they are high on intelligence are judged by their teachers and others to be creative. Their creativity should be encouraged by allowing them to work on tasks or projects that have not been planned in advance by the teacher. These students will then be able to organize material in their own fashion and practice using their unusual responses in a productive manner. Further, these children will probably arrange the project in such a way that they will keep themselves stimulated and thus work reasonably continuously on their project.

Recommendations for Students Who Are Low on Psychoticism (Tender-Minded)

Students who are low on psychoticism have a pronounced advantage in school over students with higher levels of psychoticism. For this reason, the following recommendations should be applied sparingly. They refer to procedures that will help a small number of these students deal with their peers and with schoolwork more flexibly. When over-applied in the classroom, they are ineffective.

1.   **Encourage the extremely passive child to be more assertive.**
    Students with low levels of psychoticism are not likely to be particularly dominant among their peers. At extremely low levels, these students may be very passive. In these cases (only), the teacher—possibly with the help of the school counselor—should encourage the child not to be overly compliant with peers.

2.   **Encourage independent action.**
    Students with very low levels of psychoticism are likely to follow others. In school this tendency results in conscientious work at whatever task is assigned. The child should be given the opportunity to develop and execute individual projects, although such a child will usually prefer to have the work

clearly defined by the teacher.

3. **Encourage creative responses.**

Extremely low psychotic students are not likely to produce unusual responses although these students may be very intelligent. They depend on the evaluation of the teacher and may inhibit original responses because they may be wrong. Although they prefer to be able to mark the right answer, they should be required to do some tasks that do not lead to simple right or wrong responses.

CHAPTER 9: COMBINATIONS OF THE THREE PERSONALITY DIMENSIONS

In previous chapters, each of the three personality dimensions has been discussed more or less in isolation from the others. In order to use the system to each student's full advantage, all three dimensions plus intelligence, abilities, and background, must be considered for every student. The purpose of this chapter is to demonstrate how the three dimensions can be used together.

Combinations Chart

The following chart (Fig. 9-1) is presented to illustrate the possible combinations of the three dimensions. The chart should <u>not</u> be taken to mean that there are distinct types into which all children can be classified. Each dimension is continuous and there are no points on the dimensions where the behavior of children suddenly changes. The differences along, say, the extraversion dimension are gradual, with extremely withdrawn children at the low end and only very slightly less withdrawn (or more outgoing) children at each succeeding point as we move higher on the dimension.

		P			
		Low/Middle		High	
		N		N	
		Low/Middle	High	Low/Middle	High
E	High	2. E+	5. E + N	8. E + P	11. E + PN
	Middle	1. Eo	4. N	7. P	10. PN
	Low	3. E−	6. E − N	9. E − P	12. E − PN

Figure 9-1. Combinations Chart

60

The boxes in the chart will simply allow us to focus on 12 general areas in the three-dimensional model of personality. A large number of children will be in borderline regions between two of the general areas. No attempt is made to specify firm cutoffs between areas in terms of test scores or observations (although, to be practical, approximate cutoffs are suggested in the next chapter). While these 12 boxes will organize our discussion and clarify the use of the three dimensions at the same time, using them as a rigid classification system for school children would do more harm than good.

The 12 areas are fairly arbitrarily defined. The three continuous dimensions could have been divided into any number of smaller regions. If each dimension had been divided into thirds (high, middle, and low), there would be 27 areas. On the other hand, dividing each dimension in halves (high and low) would produce eight areas. The decision to present 12 areas was based on the practical uses of each of the dimensions.

The appropriate practical divisions of the dimensions are fairly obvious for extraversion (E) and psychoticism (P), but less obvious for neuroticism (N). In the case of extraversion, the extremes show consistent intersituational approaches to social behavior and have strong characteristic differences in learning styles. The intermediate children (ambiverts) are less consistent from one situation to the next and should be considered separately. Thus, the extraversion dimension was divided into thirds. For psychoticism, the practical task is to identify those who are extremely high. In general, the middle and low levels of psychoticism can be considered together without losing information. Only very rarely will children with extremely low levels of psychoticism require special attention for that reason. Psychoticism, then, is discussed only in terms of high levels versus middle and low levels.

Neuroticism (N), at first seemed to justify division into thirds since discussing high, middle, and low levels would allow the curvilinear relationships between this dimension and performance to be reflected. However, the practical recommendations for the middle and low levels differed only minimally. For this reason and for economy, the middle and low levels of neuroticism are considered togehter. In the areas where the distinction between middle and low levels of neuroticism is critical, the distinction is made and alternate suggestions are given.

The notation in the chart shows which dimensions are above or below average for each area. E+ means extraverted and E- means introverted. Eo, or average on the extraversion dimension, is used only in the one area where no dimensions are above or below average. High psychoticism and high neuroticism are indicated by P and N, respectively. Low or middle levels of these dimensions as well as middle levels of extraversion are indicated by the absence of a P, N, or E. The numbers in the chart indicate the order in which the 12 areas are discussed.

1.   Eo

The child who is about average on the extraversion dimension and low or average on the psychoticism and neuroticism dimensions may be considered typical (Eysenck, 1967). There are far more children in this area than in any of the other 11 areas of the chart. Most researchers dealing with teaching, learning, and discipline simply assume that virtually all children are like these. In fact, research in special education, which mostly deals with intellectual, sensory, and physical differences among children, usually considers personality differences only secondarily. Consequently, there are many sources dealing with teaching and learning which can be used with these children. Some examples are given in the list of readings.

These children are usually fairly well adjusted and perform up to their capacity in school. Their behavior is flexible and reflects their immediate situation more appropriately than does the behavior of children in other areas. When they seem aggressive, anxious, introverted, or extraverted, there will be something in the school or at home that makes these behaviors adaptive. Finding the immediate environmental cause of their behavior and altering the environment brings their behavior "back to normal" fairly quickly.

In addition to environmental influences, intellectual differences determine the behavior of these children. A child with average or high intelligence will generally perform adequately in school and show few if any emotional or behavioral problems. Children whose intelligence is lower or who have a specific ability deficit will perform less well and may resent school if pushed beyond their ability or ridiculed for their performance. Adopting realistic expectations generally resolves any emotional or behavioral problems that develop (cf. Bryan & Bryan, 1975; Bush & Waugh, 1976).

Since middle and low levels of neuroticism both occur in this group of children, there are some differences in behavior within this group that reflect differences in neuroticism. Within this group, children who are higher on neuroticism—that is, about average—are well motivated and appropriately responsive to the teacher. Those who are very low on neuroticism may seem unmotivated and their performance less than would be expected for their intelligence, especially in high school and beyond. For these students, the recommendations given for students with low levels of neuroticism should be applied.

The full range of disciplinary techniques is available for these (Eo) children. Praise (or reward or reinforcement) and punishment are both effective with these children, although if either is overused the other will be more effective (Brophy & Evertson, 1976). The most effective disciplinary strategy would seem to include using praise and punishment about equally.

Since most teachers prefer using praise, some reassurance about punishment is appropriate. Recent reviews of punishment (e.g., Walters & Grusec, 1977) have demonstrated that punishment is effective. In fact, it seems to have stronger effects on behavior than does reward. Also, contrary to popular psychology (which unfortunately influences the thinking of many professional psychologists), punishment used consistently seems to result in no emotional side effects. Punishment should be administered privately to avoid having classmates think of the child as a troublemaker, and possibly encouraging the behavior the teacher is trying to inhibit.

When using rewards with these children, social rewards such as verbal praise, are usually more effective than material rewards such as toys or candy (Stevenson, 1972). In fact, material rewards should probably only be used with deprived (poor or institutionalized) children who have no other way of obtaining them. Children of parents who encourage good performance in school do better work when their best work is sent home for their parents to see. For these children, getting the parents to sign a good paper (and of course the attention and approval that go with it) is far more motivating than even praise from the teacher. Unfortunately, if the parents are not interested in the child's schoolwork, having them sign papers is completely without value.

With the typical (Eo) child, the teacher should use stimulating techniques with very easy (for the child) material, particularly when the child is also very low on neuroticism, and less stimulating techniques with difficult material. This will take advantage of the relationship between arousal level and performance that was discussed in the chapters on extraversion and neuroticism.

The teacher can also control the difficulty level of tests and exercises in order to maximize the academic achievement of these children. Although the advocates of mastery learning seem to advise using material that is very easy for the child, so that mistakes are rarely made, evidence (Good, Biddle, & Brophy, 1975) indicates that students have their highest achievement levels when their work allows them to answer from 70 to 80 percent of the items correctly. Apparently, if the typical student is right much more often than about 80 percent of the time, the child is not challenged by the material, loses interest, and does not spend as much time or effort studying as otherwise would be the case. On the other hand, if the child is right much less than 70 percent of the time, he or she may give up, once again studying less than would otherwise be the case. For typical students, the optimal difficulty of the material allows them to respond correctly 70 to 80 percent of the time. This figure will be adjusted for students in the other groups that will be discussed.

The full range of instructional techniques is appropriate for these children (cf. Dunkin & Biddle, 1974). They are flexible enough to take full advantage of group work and individual assignments. Lecture can be used to present specific information, and discussion to stimulate interest in material. Although exercises that allow children to discover principles and applications on their own should occasionally be presented, a well structured approach will produce the greatest achievement in the long run.

It should be noted that individual variation in personality has not been eliminated in this group, only reduced. All children who fit in this group will not behave in exactly the same ways. While the most extreme variations in behavior among these children result from variables outside the domain of personality, such as intelligence and situational variables, some variation on the three personality dimensions remains. In fact, there are children near the outer boundaries of this group whose behavior and learning styles have points in common with every other group shown in the chart.

For those children in this area of the chart who are close to another area, the recommendations appropriate to that area should be considered. If they seem appropriate, they should be applied. The continued application of any special recommendations—should be dependent on the results obtained in achievement, behavior, and attitudes toward school. Carefully used, the recommendations for nearby areas of the chart can increase the teacher's chances of finding the best ways of dealing with every child.

2.   E+

Students who are high on the extraversion dimension and moderate or low on the neuroticism and psychoticism dimensions are sociable and uninhibited (Eysenck, 1967). Recommendations for students with high levels of extraversion have been presented previously and can be applied to this group of children without modification. These children are usually fairly well adjusted, showing no behavior or emotional problems. In fact, their outgoing, sociable behavior may make them seem, if anything, even better adjusted than the typical (Eo) child. On the other hand, their tendencies to talk loudly and frequently and to respond impulsively require some attention from the teacher.

When neuroticism is extremely low for a child in this group, the child may seem unmotivated to do schoolwork and extremely difficult to interest in academic work. Such a child will probably be likable and there will be little suggestion of a "psychological" problem. When one of these children is also fairly bright, a considerable degree of skill may be developed in manipulating the teacher to get out of schoolwork. Of course, if the child is generally successful at manipulating the teacher, school performance will decline. For children with high extraversion and very low neuroticism, extremely stimulating material and a liberal use of praise should produce the best performance. The material presented to these children should be somewhat easier than that presented to the typical (Eo) child in order to increase the frequency of answering correctly, and thereby being rewarded.

3.   E-

Students who are low on extraversion and moderate or low on the neuroticism and psychoticism dimensions are shy and inhibit their responses (Eysenck, 1967). Recommendations for students with low extraversion have been presented previously and can be applied without modification. These children are usually fairly well adjusted, showing few if any emotional or behavior problems, except in response to being made the center of attention too suddenly or too frequently.

Since most teachers, especially elementary teachers, value outgoing sociable behavior, they may suspect emotional problems in these children. Actually, in this area which includes only middle and lower levels of neuroticism, anxiety or fear of school are unusual unless the teacher calls the child to the attention of other students frequently or emphasizes social interaction too strongly. Although it is hard for many teachers to believe, these children (E-) can be socially withdrawn and yet be happy and productive in school.

Since middle and low levels of neuroticism occur in this area, some differences in behavior within this group are attributable to differences in neuroticism.

While those students who are higher on neuroticism (about average) may be more motivated to do schoolwork, even the ones with lower levels of neuroticism are alert and cooperative. All the children in this area respond well to schoolwork when presented as a serious undertaking.

These children will work diligently and can be given assignments that are somewhat more difficult than would be given to typical (Eo) students. Slightly more difficult material emphasizes the seriousness of school for these children, and increases the frequency of incorrect responses, that provide information these students can use. If the additional difficulty results in slower responding, the teacher can tell the child not to worry about missing items and to answer faster. These children should respond well to such instructions as long as they are working privately. In public situations, on the other hand, easy questions produce the most uninhibited responses from these children and can be used to increase the frequency of their talking in front of the class.

4.   N

Students who are high on neuroticism, average on extraversion, and average or low on psychoticism are emotionally overreactive (Eysenck, 1967). Recommendations for students with high neuroticism have been presented previously. These recommendations can be applied as stated. These students have a high incidence of emotional problems such as test anxiety, school phobias, and low self-esteem. They seldom show disruptive behavior problems, although they may have emotional outbursts in response to specific stressful or threatening situations.

These students are usually highly motivated to perform well in school, and they are very sensitive to praise and threats of punishment. Their behavior is fairly easy to control, leading them to become over-controlled.

Differences in behavior among children in this group arise primarily from intellectual and situational factors. Children in this group (N) who are highly intelligent will be able, well-motivated, or even driven students. They will spend a great deal of time and effort on schoolwork although they may not like schoolwork. On the other hand, those who are less intelligent than average may have a severe lack of self-esteem. These students are also highly motivated to perform well and usually believe that school performance is very important. Their repeated failure to perform well leads to frustration and lowered self-esteem. They often become fearful of school and resist being involved in new situations that may lead to further failure.

Situational factors have extremely strong effects on the behavior of these children. In very unstressful, nonthreatening situations, the behavior of these children (N) differs hardly at all from the behavior of typical (Eo) children. As the environmental stress increases, the differences increase, putting the highly neurotic children at a progressively greater disadvantage. Also, these children will react more strongly to the teacher's behavior than will other children. When the teacher uses disciplinary and instructional techniques to obtain appropriate behavior from typical children, highly neurotic children will seem to overreact.

5.   E+N

Students with high levels of extraversion and neuroticism and low or average levels of psychoticism may be described as hyperactive. These children are outgoing and uninhibited as well as anxious and overreactive (Eysenck, 1967). The recommendations presented for students with high levels of extraversion and those for students high on neuroticism should both be applied to these children. In fact, the reader with a background in the field of learning disabilities (cf. Bryan & Bryan, 1975) will recognize that these two sets of recommendations taken together are very similar to recommendations for managing hyperactives that have been developed by workers in that field.

The inconsistencies in both sets of recommendations should be pointed out. Many of the recommendations for highly extraverted students are based on those students' relatively low levels of arousal. Stimulation and moderate stress were recommended to increase their arousal. Some of the recommendations for highly neurotic students, on the other hand, were designed to prevent these emotionally overreactive children from becoming too highly aroused to perform well. This inconsistency reflects the behavior of hyperactive children whose performance improves when they are aroused either with stimulating materials or stimulant drugs, but who have a tendency to show "catastrophic" emotional overreaction.

Resolving these inconsistencies requires that the teacher use materials and social interaction to arouse the child rather than strong emotional stimulation. Although both praise and threats of punishment are effective with these children (E+N), they have different undesirable effects with them. Praise or other reward may have such a strong effect that it distracts the child from the task at hand. Threats of punishment, while moderately effective, must occasionally be followed by actual punishment for these relatively impulsive children in order to maintain their credibility. Actual punishment of these children will lead to overreaction and decreased academic performance. The difficulties involved in maintaining discipline with these students are familiar to most teachers. The teacher who uses praise while constantly redirecting the child's attention to the task is most successful with these children.

6.   E-N

Students who are low on extraversion, high on neuroticism, and low or average on psychoticism are best described as anxious (Eysenck, 1967). These emotionally overreactive, yet quiet, children are usually extremely cautious. The recommendations for students with low extraversion and those for students with high neuroticism should be applied with these children.

Both sets of recommendations should be given heavy emphasis with these children. The recommendations for students with low levels of extraversion (introverts) were based on these students' high levels of arousal. A very little environmental stimulation pushes these students past their optimal performance levels. In fact, reducing the arousal of these students is usually beneficial. Similarly, the easily aroused, highly neurotic students are also readily overstimulated. When low extraversion and high neuroticism (E-N) occur in the same child, the child is usually far too aroused (anxious) to perform well in school. Any steps taken to reduce anxiety will be in the right direction, although strong and consistent emphasis on reducing arousal is necessary to improve performance substantially.

The quiet, reserved behavior of these children (except when upset) may not give the teacher a strong sign that special attention is necessary. They will attempt to avoid a large variety of things that other children do not find frightening and may even like. Often they attempt to avoid school entirely by demonstrating their fear. Treatment of these "school phobics" requires desensitization (by a trained psychologist) of many of their specific fears at school as well as the anticipation of future anxiety-arousing situations they may encounter at school. Gradual presentation of these situations to the child will allow him to avoid becoming immobilized with fear.

7.   P

Students with high levels of psychoticism, average levels of extraversion, and average or low levels of neuroticism are likely to have behavior problems that disrupt class (Eysenck & Eysenck, 1976). They are also likely to attempt to dominate their classmates through aggressive acts. Recommendations for students with high levels of psychoticism have been presented previously and can be applied with this group of children without modification. These children are difficult to control with either rewards or punishment. Their continual sensation seeking leads to disruptive behavior, but can, with some effort, be used to enhance their academic performance.

Since neuroticism varies from low to average levels in this group, there are some differences in behavior resulting from differences in neuroticism. Those with extremely low levels of neuroticism are likely to be very cold toward other people. These children are usually more competent at their misdeeds, probably because they develop less anxiety and guilt over them than do those with higher levels of neuroticism. Those with higher (about average) levels of neuroticism act out somewhat more often than those with lower neuroticism, but they are more responsive to disciplinary measures and usually carry out their serious misdeeds less competently than do those with lower levels of neuroticism.

Children with high levels of psychoticism are relatively insensitive to moderate variations in situational factors. They try to excite themselves in any situation and do not seem to change their behavior to adapt to the consequences whether the consequences are natural, such as being hit by a car, or imposed as punishment by a parent or teacher. While extremely stressfull situations may make these children become suddenly disoriented (break), and experiences in their past may have contributed to their current high levels of psychoticism, moderate disciplinary measures such as a teacher might use have small effects on their behavior.

Most differences in behavior within this group are attributable to intellectual factors. Children in this group (P) with high intelligence are likely to be very original, creative students. They are not the most pleasant students to work with, but teachers often recognize their promise. Children with lower intelligence are less able to direct their unusual behavior toward productive ends. A great deal of effort is necessary to maintain discipline and promote academic achievement with these children.

8.   E+P

Students with high levels of extraversion and psychoticism and average or low levels of neuroticism are extremely impulsive (S. Eysenck & Eysenck, 1977). Their behavior is directed toward other people, often violently. The recommendations for students with high levels of psychoticism and those for students with high levels of extraversion should be applied with these children.

Several of the recommendations in the two sets are similar, particularly those involving the use of stimulating materials and those concerning impulsivity. The recommendations regarding impulsivity are particularly important for this group of children, and particular attention should be given to applying them. The recommendations for using stimulating techniques and materials were developed with different rationales. For high extraversion, stimulating materials raise the child's usually low arousal level, allowing him to perform better. For high psychoticism, stimulating experiences should serve as rewards following good work. These children will work in order to be stimulated. When the same child has high extraversion and high psychoticism, stimulation both during work and as a consequence of good work are necessary for optimal performance.

The differences in behavior within this group arising from differences in neuroticism, intelligence, and situational factors are similar to the differences in the P group. Children in this group (E+P) should respond somewhat better to the use of rewards than to the use of punishment, although their response to either is minimal.

9.   E-P

Students who have low levels of extraversion, high levels of psychoticism, and low or average levels of neuroticism are withdrawn and hostile (Eysenck & Eysenck, 1976). Their hostile behavior is usually directed at things rather than at people, making vandalism a more common misbehavior than physical aggression among these children. The recommendations for students with low levels of extraversion and high levels of psychoticism may be applied with these children. However, some qualifications must be made for this group.

With regard to impulsive responding, these children (E-P) are likely to be unpredictable, sometimes responding impulsively and sometimes seeming overly cautious in their responses. Recommendations regarding impulsivity and cautiousness are contradictory for low extraversion and high psychoticism. While following one of the recommendations, the teacher should be especially careful not to push the child to the other extreme of impulsivity or caution, both of which are detrimental to school performance.

The recommendations for high levels of psychoticism that deal with competitiveness, social interaction, and allowing the child to act as a leader are not appropriate when the child is also low on extraversion. These children are likely to experience being called to the attention of other children as punishing, rather than rewarding.

These children are not as likely to engage in aggressive behavior as they are to steal or destroy objects. This is consistent with the tendency of introverts to try to avoid punishment. Similarly, threats of punishment from a teacher are more effective than rewards for controlling the behavior of these children. However, both will be relatively ineffective, and when punishment is actually administered, it is likely to have the effect of increasing the undesired behavior rather than suppressing it, since intense stimulation is rewarding for these students.

Stimulating techniques should be applied only at certain times with this group. Since they are low on extraversion, stimulation during their work can be expected to interfere with their performance. On the other hand, since they are high on psychoticism, strong stimulation resulting from (that is, after) their work is highly rewarding and will increase the amount and quality of their future work. Of course, after this stimulation, their arousal levels must be reduced before they can continue to perform well. Practically, these students should have material presented in a subdued manner and be followed by exciting consequences. If possible, the excitement should be administered before a naturally occurring break, such as lunch, recess, or the end of the school day, so the child will not have to continue work in an overstimulated state.

Differences within this group due to differences in neuroticism, intelligence, and situational factors are similar to those discussed for the P group.

10. PN

Students with high levels of psychoticism and neuroticism and middle levels of extraversion are likely to be frequently or continually agitated (Eysenck & Eysenck, 1976). The recommendations for students with high psychoticism and those for students with high neuroticism can be applied with these students.

These students have emotional and behavioral problems in combination. Since they are high on psychoticism, they participate in sensation seeking activities without concern for the consequences. As high neurotics, they overreact to emotional stimulation which frequently results from their activities. This feedback keeps them in a nearly continual state of over-stimulation and anxiety. Just as they are not likely to do very well academically, their high neuroticism also keeps them from being competent even at their misdeeds. While they strike out emotionally frequently, they do not usually have the foresight or stability to execute a serious misdeed successfully (Eysenck & Eysenck, 1976).

Practically, the teacher's primary tasks with these children are to avoid overarousing them and to prevent them from overarousing themselves. The teacher will probably need, and should not hesitate to request, help from a psychologist for these children.

11. E+PN

Students who are at high levels on all three personality dimensions have the highest frequencies of disruptive behavior of all 12 groups (Eysenck & Eysenck,

1976). The three sets of recommendations for students high on all the dimensions will be appropriate for these students, although some problems will arise in actually applying them.

The stimulating texhniques used to arouse students high on extraversion and reward students high on psychoticism may be used with these students as long as they do not involve stressful or emotional components. Talking loudly in a threatening manner to one of these children is likely to result in emotional overreaction and physical aggression, probably directed toward the teacher.

Practically, the teacher's task is similar to the task with the previous group (PN). In addition, these children (E+PN) will be even more impulsive and aggressive. The teacher will probably need outside help with one of these students. Teachers should in no sense feel that they have failed to do their job when they cannot keep up with the individual needs of about 30 students, prepare for from one to six subjects (for students with different abilities), and give their constant attention to controlling the behavior of a highly unusual child.

12. E-PN

Students with high levels of psychoticism and neuroticism and low levels of extraversion are very anxious and agitated. They are similar to the PN and E+PN groups but more anxious and less physically aggressive than either of these groups (Eysenck & Eysenck, 1976). The recommendations for students with high psychoticism, for high neuroticism, and for low extraversion are generally appropriate for these students.

For these children, stimulation during work should be strictly avoided. Even stimulation as a consequence of good work may increase the child's arousal far beyond the point of optimal performance.

The treatment of children in this group is similar to that of children in the PN group except that they are less likely to be openly aggressive and are more anxious and fearful than children in that group; thus, more attention should be given to reducing anxiety and somewhat less to controlling aggression. Their behavior may be erratic, alternating between fearful withdrawing and emotional, but usually ineffectual, striking out. In general, the teacher should avoid stimulating such a child and obtain outside psychological help as soon as possible.

Summary

The combinations of, and interactions among, the three personality dimensions on learning and behavior were discussed. A chart of 12 combinations of personality dimensions was presented. Suggestions for optimal teaching and disciplinary procedures were discussed for each of the 12 combinations.

Readings for "Combinations"
Brophy, J. E., & Evertson, C. M. *Learning from teaching: A developmental perspective.* Boston: Allyn & Bacon, 1976.

Bryan, T. H., & Bryan, J. H. *Understanding learning disabilities.* Port Washington, NY: Alfred, 1975.

Bush, W. J., & Waugh, K. W. *Diagnosing learning disabilities.* Columbus, OH: Merrill, 1976.

Dunkin, M. J., & Biddle, B. J. *The study of teaching.* New York: Holt, Rinehart & Winston, 1974.

Eysenck, H. J. *The biological basis of personality.* Springfield, IL: Thomas, 1967.

Eysenck, H. J., & Eysenck, S. B. G. *Psychoticism as a dimension of personality.* London: Hodder & Stoughton, 1976.

Eysenck, S. B. G., & Eysenck, H. J. The place of impulsiveness in a dimensional system of personality description. *British Journal of Social and Clinical Psychology,* 1977, *16*, 57-68.

Glasser, A. J., & Zimmerman, I. L. *Clinical interpretation of the Wechsler Intelligence Scale for Children.* New York: Grune & Stratton, 1967.

Good, T. L., Biddle, B. J., & Brophy, J. E. *Teachers make a difference.* New York: Holt, Rinehart & Winston, 1975.

Stevenson, H. W. *Children's learning.* Englewood Cliffs, NJ: Prentice-Hall, 1972.

Walters, G. C., & Grusec, J. E. *Punishment.* San Francisco: Freeman, 1977.

CHAPTER 10: MEASUREMENT OF THE THREE PERSONALITY DIMENSIONS

A psychologist, counselor, or teacher who is interested in using information about a student's personality to improve instructional and disciplinary procedures used with that student needs techniques for assessing the three personality dimensions. Fortunately, the extraversion, neuroticism, and psychoticism dimensions are such broad, common factors of human behavior that they appear in virtually all personality questionnaires and behavior checklists. Evidence of the three dimensions may also be seen in a large variety of cognitive (intelligence and ability) tests. Extreme examples of these dimensions, such as an extremely extraverted student, can be identified by almost anyone. After becoming thoroughly familiar with the dimensions and observing a reasonably large, say 100, and representative sample of students, many teachers may become skillful in making rough assessments that may be adequate in most cases. In fact, the best teachers already use some personality differences to guide instruction, although in an unsystematic and less completely effective manner than is possible.

Several methods of assessing these three dimensions will be presented. The *Junior Eysenck Personality Questionnaire* (Eysenck & Eysenck, 1975) is the primary instrument used by psychologists and counselors and will be covered first. For those who currently use other personality and interest tests, a few of these will be discussed as measures of the three dimensions. Finally, indicators of the three dimensions that can be obtained from the Wechsler intelligence scales will be presented.

Junior Eysenck Personality Questionnaire (JEPQ)

The JEPQ (Eysenck & Eysenck, 1975) consists of a list of 81 statements to be answered "yes" or "no" by the child. In most cases, it should take less than half an hour to administer the questionnaire. There are four scales on the JEPQ: psychoticism (P), extraversion (E), neuroticism (N), and a lie (L) scale.

The JEPQ has been standardized on boys and girls between the ages of 7 and 15, although the limited reliabilities of the scales for ages 7, 8, and 9 make its use with children of these ages questionable. The reliabilities of the scales for children age 10 and older are adequate for measures of personality; however, even at these ages the reliabilities are mostly in the .70s and .80s. The JEPQ should be used only by a trained psychologist who has an adequate background in measurement, personality, and children's learning. The abnormal sounding names of two of the scales and the error contained in each scale could result in damage to the child if used in an unsophisticated manner.

For students above the age of 15, the *Eysenck Personality Questionnaire* (EPQ) can be used. The EPQ, with 90 items, is very similar to the JEPQ and is somewhat more reliable. Most of the reliabilities are in the .80s. Users of either the EPQ or the JEPQ should become familiar with the manual and the material in this book, and ideally with the material presented in *Personality Structure and Measurement* (Eysenck & Eysenck, 1969), *The Biological Basis of Personality* (Eysenck, 1967) and *Psychoticism as a Dimension of Personality* (Eysenck & Eysenck, 1976), before attempting to interpret or make recommendations from these instruments.

It should be noted that the JEPQ and the EPQ questionnaires and their norms were developed in Britain; however, since American norm supplements are available, there should be no practical problem with using them. Furthermore, the differences between the American and British norms are very small, and a large body of cross-cultural research indicates that the three personality dimensions are generally related to similar learning and behavior characteristics in Europe, North America, Australia, Africa, the Near East, and the Far East (cf. Eysenck, 1967; Eysenck & Eysenck, 1976).

The validity of the scales of the JEPQ and EPQ for measuring the three dimensions is a strong point. Most of the research on personality and learning has used either these instruments or their predecessors, which are very similar. A vast amount of material relating these questionnaires with learning, cognitive styles, effects of therapy, and other variables is presented in the chapter readings or can be traced from these sources. Eysenck (1967) and Eysenck and Eysenck (1976) are particularly helpful.

In practical use, the JEPQ (or the EPQ) can be administered either individually or in a group. Although the measurement characteristics do not differ between individual and group administration, individual administration will allow the psychologist to discuss answers to individual items and pursue clinical hunches in order to produce a more detailed account of the child's current behavior patterns. When this information is included with intelligence, ability, and achievement information about the child, the psychologist can suggest ways of capitalizing on or modifying the child's behavior to produce optimal learning and adjustment.

Using the JEPQ to Individualize Instruction

In order to relate the child's scores on the JEPQ to the recommendations presented in this book, it is suggested that a score of about one standard deviation above the mean for the child's age group be used to distinguish between high scores and middle or average scores. (The number of points in a standard deviation on each of the scales is given in the manual. Readers interested in technical definitions of terms such as "standard deviation," "mean," "reliability," and "validity" should consult Anastasi [1976] or any other book on psychological testing.) A score of about one standard deviation below the mean will distinguish between the low and middle ranges of each dimension. These "cut-off scores" are not meant to be used in a rigid manner. Differences in behavior along the three dimensions are gradual and no sharp division between, say, extraverts and ambiverts is possible.

The child's lie (L) score should be considered very carefully in arriving at an assessment of personality (Eysenck & Eysenck, 1976). The L score has moderate, negative correlations with both psychoticism (P) and neuroticism (N). It is unrelated to the extraversion (E) score. If a child's L score is within about a standard deviation of the mean (or even lower), scores on P, E, and N may be considered fairly accurate. If, however, a child's L score is more than about a standard deviation above the mean, the P score or the N score (or both) will be lower than it should be. While no formal correction for the L scale will be offered, the questionnaire user should consider the recommendations offered for children with higher P and/or higher N scores as possible recommendations for the child with a high L score. These recommendations must be applied tentatively since we will not be sure, for an individual student, whether the high L score masks a higher P score, a higher N score, or both higher P and N scores than those obtained.

After taking the child's L score into account, the questionnaire user should decide which, if any, of the P, E, and N scales are high or low and consider the recommendations presented in previous chapters for high and low scores on these dimensions. The child should then be placed tentatively into one of the areas in the chart (Fig. 9-1) presented in the "combinations" chapter. Additional suggestions made for the child's group and for similar groups in the chart should be considered.

The recommendations appropriate for any one child may be fairly numerous. It is not necessary to implement all of the suggestions at once. Because of constraints imposed by the physical or administrative structure of the school or by the teacher's preferences, some of the recommendations will be impossible (or very difficult) to implement. Implement the convenient recommendations first. Only when these do not produce adequate results should the psychologist or teacher insist on applying the less convenient recommendations.

It is important to remember that personality information should always be used along with intelligence, ability, and achievement information plus background and situational information, to develop appropriate instructional and disciplinary plans for a child. Having stated this, we will list the steps involved in using the JEPQ for instructional planning. While the use of other sources of information is mentioned in only one step, this does not reflect the relative importance of personality and cognitive or background information, but only the focus of the book in hand. The steps are:

1. Administer and score the JEPQ (or EPQ).
2. Decide whether L is higher than about +1.0 S.D.
3. If it is, consider the P and N scores to be underestimated and proceed as if they were slightly higher than they are.
4. Identify high or low P, E, or N scores (greater than +1.0 S.D. or less than -1.0 S.D.).
5. Consider the recommendations appropriate to the child's high or low scores presented in the chapters on using each of the three dimensions to individualize instruction.
6. Place the child in an area in the combinations chart (Fig. 9-1) and consider suggestions for that combination.
7. Consider recommendations for areas in the combinations chart that are similar in terms of P, E, or N (that is, nearby areas in the chart).
8. Check the child's scores to make sure that rigid application of "cut-off scores" has not artificially eliminated possible recommendations.
9. Consider other information—intelligence, abilities, achievement, attitudes, background—about the child.
10. Consider situational constraints, including the teacher's preferences in classroom procedures.
11. Implement the recommendations that are (a) appropriate for the child and (b) reasonably convenient.
12. Evaluate the success of the recommendations with the teacher's judgment of the child's improvement in schoolwork and behavior.
13. Depending on the previous evaluation, either continue the application of the recommendations or implement different recommendations.

Example: Ten-Year-Old Girl

As an example, let us consider a ten-year-old (fifth grade) girl with about average school achievement, and no measureable ability deficits. Her scores on the JEPQ are -.5 S.D. (half a standard deviation below the mean) on P, -.8 S.D. on E, +.1 S.D. on N, and +.1 S.D. on L. Her JEPQ scores are shown in the following figure (10-1). First, we notice that her L score is very close to average. Next, we notice that her scores on P, E, and N are within a standard deviation (between +1.0 S.D. and -1.0 S.D.) of the mean. None of the recommendations for high and low scorers are considered relevant (for the moment). In the combinations chart (Fig. 9-1), her near average scores place her in the Eo (typical) group. The suggestions for this group are then compared with her teacher's usual classroom practices. If there are marked discrepancies between these suggestions and her teacher's practices, the teacher may adjust her treatment of this one child in order to bring about an improvement in her achievement.

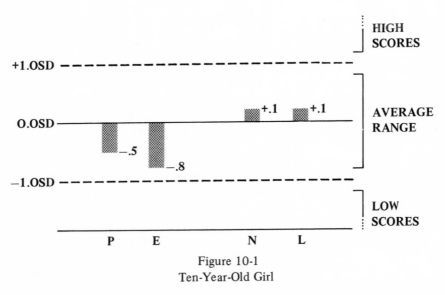

Figure 10-1
Ten-Year-Old Girl

This student's fairly low (-.8 S.D.) score on extraversion places her near the E- (introverted) group in the combinations chart. Suggestions appropriate for this group and for students with low extraversion can be considered as additional possibilities for this child. Particularly, if no discrepancies between the Eo suggestions and her teacher's practices are found (or if discrepancies are found but cannot reasonably be corrected), suggestions for the nearby E- group can be tentatively applied.

After the recommendations are applied, her classroom performance and behavior should be closely monitored for signs of improvement or deterioration. The recommendations are to be continued or discontinued based on the teacher's (not the psychologist's) judgment of whether her performance has improved, deteriorated, or stayed about the same during the period following the implementation of the recommendations. Since these recommendations can have an effect on standardized achievement tests only when applied over an extended period of time, the teacher's judgment is the best indication of the immediate effects of newly implemented procedures.

Other Personality Instruments

The three personality dimensions under discussion, especially extraversion and neuroticism, are widely agreed to be factors occurring on virtually all personality inventories and behavioral observations (cf. Wiggins, 1968). Any of the hundreds of personality inventories and behavior checklists now being used in clinical or research work could be scored for the three factors. Two personality instruments and one behavior checklist have been selected for discussion as measures of the three dimensions. However, a psychologist who already has another favorite "test" should have little difficulty identifying the three factors in it. The three to be discussed here are *Cattell's Sixteen Personality Factors Questionnaire*, the *Minnesota Multiphasic Personality Inventory*, and Kohn's behavior checklists.

The *Sixteen Personality Factors Questionnaire* (16PF) (Cattell et al., 1970) is a personaltiy questionnaire developed for use with adults. Downward extensions of the 16PF are the *High School Personality Questionnaire* (HSPQ), for ages 12 through 18; the *Children's Personality Questionnaire* (CPQ), for ages 9 through 12; and the *Early School Personality Questionnaire* (ESPQ), for ages 6 through 8. The 16PF has scales for measuring 16 personality factors and the downward extensions have somewhat fewer scales. All of these instruments can be scored for second-order factors (that is, more general factors) called Extraversion, Anxiety, Tough Poise, Independence, and Sociopathy.

Cattell's second-order factors are roughly equivalent to Eysenck's three factors. Cattell's inventories can be used instead of Eysenck's to individualize instruction, although the author prefers Eysenck's questionnaires because (a) more of the learning research has used them and (b) they are shorter. In order to use Cattell's instruments, the relationship between the two sets of factors must be considered. Cattell's Extraversion and Eysenck's Extraversion are equivalent. Cattell's Anxiety can be treated as equivalent to Eysenck's Neuroticism, although Eysenck and Eysenck (1969) consider Anxiety a combination of Neuroticism and (low) Extraversion. Cattell's last three second-order factors seem to measure different aspects of Psychoticism.

The practical use of Cattell's measures involves the same steps presented in the previous section except that Cattell's Extraversion will be used for E, Anxiety for N, and an average of Tough Poise, Independence, and Sociopathy for P. The user of Cattell's instruments should become familiar with the material concerning them in the list of readings. Cattell and Scheier (1961) and Eysenck and Eysenck (1969), in particular, contain information dealing with the relationship between the two systems.

The *Minnesota Multiphasic Personality Inventory* (MMPI) (Marks et al., 1974) is a widely used personality questionnaire. Although constructed for adults, it is used with adolescents as young as 14 (and occasionally younger). The MMPI is used to identify pathology and should be used only by psychologists with extensive training in personality, measurement, and the use of the MMPI, specifically. While its use by a school psychologist is rare, it is frequently given to adolescents by private clinicians. These clinicians can suggest to a teacher the recommendations in this book from the personality information from the MMPI. The three personality factors discussed in this book can be estimated by the following rules, in which Eysenck's factors are on the left sides of the equations and MMPI scales are on the right:

1. $P = (Pa + Pt + Sc)/3$
2. $E = (-Si)$
3. $N = (Hs + D + Hy)/3$

These rules give P, E, and N in the T scores that are familiar to clinicians who use the MMPI. Scores between about 40 and about 60 should be considered average on each dimension, and those above 60 and below 40 should be considered high and low, respectively. The E score can be further checked by considering the MMPI Ma score, which is a combination of E and N, and the MMPI Pd score, which is a combination of E and P. If both these scores are high (or low) together, especially if the other scores in the rules above are not high (or low), this is additional evidence of high (or low) E. The MMPI Pd and Ma scores can also be used as further evidence for P and N, respectively. Several readings that will be helpful in using the MMPI to individualize instruction are Eysenck (1976), Eysenck & Eysenck (1976), Wakefield et al. (1974), and Wakefield et al. (1975).

Behavior checklists filled out by a parent or a teacher are becoming common in assessing emotional and behavior problems of children. Most of these checklists measure two syndromes, or traits, that are very similar to psychoticism (behavior problems) and neuroticism (emotional problems) as discussed herein. Although there are a large number of them, the checklists presented by Kohn (1977) are particularly interesting. He successfully measured two factors that he called apathy-withdrawal (neuroticism) and anger-defiance (psychoticism) using two different kinds of checklists. One checklist, the *Social Competence Scale,* used ratings of positive (competent) behavior. The other, the *Symptoms Checklist,* used ratings of negative behavior (symptoms). Both produced similar factors which were similarly negatively related to academic achievement during the period from preschool to the fourth grade. Kohn's review of other rating systems in clinical work with children is consistent with the use of psychoticism and neuroticism as separate factors.

Wechsler Scales

Three intelligence scales by Wechsler are widely used with school children. They are the *Wechsler Preschool and Primary Scale of Intelligence* (WPPSI), the *Wechsler Intelligence Scale for Children—Revised* (WISC-R), and the *Wechsler Adult Intelligence Scale* (WAIS). The WISC-R (Wechsler, 1974) is by far the most widely used in schools since the age range of this test covers almost the entire age range of public schools. The other two are used for the extremely early and late school years. While the present discussion will focus on the WISC-R, the comments apply equally well to the WPPSI and WAIS.

Several books (e.g., Glasser & Zimmerman, 1967) contain suggestions for obtaining personality information from the Wechsler scales. The present discussion is not intended to review these suggestions but to organize them in terms of P, E, and N. This will allow psychologists who obtain personality information from the WISC-R to use it to arrive at specific recommendations for improving the student's classroom performance.

The WISC-R is a highly reliable instrument (reliabilities consistently in the .90s) that predicts quality of schoolwork and time to master specific objectives about as well as any measure (correlations ranging from about .50 to about .70) available for school age children. Although currently criticized for discriminating against ethnic minorities and economically disadvantaged students, the differences among these groups on the WISC-R accurately reflect differences in the academic achievement of these groups, and prediction of academic achievement is the *sine qua non* of intelligence measures.

The WISC-R consists of 12 test that sample a wide variety of intellectual behavior. Some tests—Information, Arithmetic, and Vocabulary—are very similar to actual schoolwork. Other tests measure characteristics that are important in schoolwork, but are not as likely to be examined apart from other abilities in class as they are on the WISC-R. Immediate memory (Digit Span test), attention to detail (Picture Comprehension), sustained effort (Coding), verbal expressiveness (Comprehension), spatial organization (Block Design), and higher-order conceptualization (Similarities) are some of these characteristics.

While administering the WISC-R, the psychologist can closely observe the child's behavior at tasks that many other children have been observed to perform. Not only does the quality of children's performance on these tasks vary, but the way they approach the tasks and react to the examiner vary. These observations can be used by an experienced psychologist to estimate the three personality dimensions for a child.

Observations relevant to P include fantastic, unusual, or bizarre responses on any of the tests. The child with high P may express hostility or cruelty on any of the verbal tests and respond impulsively on any of the performance (non-verbal) tests. This child will not seem to plan actions on the Picture Arrangement and Mazes tests as others do. Such a child may also have difficulty establishing set on Picture Completion, give over inclusive responses on Similarities, and be resistant to the Arithmetic test. If a child shows several of these behaviors, the recommendations for students with high psychoticism should be considered.

The child with very low P will tend to be very obedient and cooperative. Such a child will not show any of the behaviors in the preceding paragraph and may give fairly concrete responses on Similarities.

The child with high E will generally behave in a friendlier manner than is typical. On the verbal tasks high E children will mention friends more frequently and, especially on Comprehension and Picture Arrangement, emphasize the rewarding (as opposed to the punishing) aspects of situations. They will tend toward impulsivity, distractibility, and acting without planning on the performance tests. The recommendations for students with high extraversion should be considered for these children.

At the other extreme, the introverted (low E) child will generally be less friendly. On the verbal tasks, low E children will talk about things or about people in an impersonal manner and emphasize the punishing possibilities of situations. They will plan before responding and tend to be hesitant and thoughtful. They are likely to show more disappointment after missing an item than is typical. The recommendations for students with low extraversion should be considered for these children.

Children with high N show their anxiety and tension in a number of ways. Throughout the WISC-R, they will give overly detailed responses, while often neglecting essential details in the stimulus material. They will seem distractible and apprehensive. They often show a pattern of missing easy items and passing harder ones, particularly on the Information test, and making unexpectedly low scores on Arithmetic, while scoring higher on paper and pencil arithmetic tests. They are more disturbed by the pressure of the timed tests and perform by trial and error on easier items than other children. They may also shuffle the pieces nervously on the Block Design and Object Assembly tests. On Coding they will either perform extremely well or will try to make each symbol so perfectly that they do very badly on the test. They often seem to "try too hard." The recommendations for students with high neuroticism should be considered for these children.

On the other hand, children with very low N seem not to try at all. They are more relaxed than usual during testing. They do not show any of the behaviors mentioned in the previous paragraph, but may show large differences between the forward and backward parts of the Digit Span test as well as poor lethargic performance on Coding. The recommendations for students with low N should be considered for these children.

The observations made with the WISC-R do not differ substantially from observations that an alert teacher, experienced with children and very familiar with the specific instructional materials being used, could make in the classroom. Although a psychologist will be able to observe the child without being distracted by the other pressing responsibilities a teacher has, a teacher can make accurate observations in the classroom similar to those discussed with the WISC-R. These observations should then be followed with the appropriate recommendations presented in the previous chapters of this book.

Summary

Techniques for measuring the three personality dimensions and procedures for implementing recommendations presented in previous chapters were discussed. Several personality instruments, and primarily the JEPQ, can be used to measure children's personality. Personality can also be assessed by direct behavioral observation by those with proper training and experience. An observation system for use with the Wechsler intelligence scales was discussed. Implementation of teaching recommendations from personality information requires careful consideration of the student's abilities and background, constraints imposed by the school, and the teacher's preferences and time limitations.

Readings for "Measurement"
Anastasi, A. *Psychological testing (4th Ed.).* New York: Macmillan, 1976.
Cattell, R. B., & Cattell, M. D. L. *Handbook for the Jr.-Sr. High School Personality Questionnaire.* Champaign, IL: Institute for Personality and Ability Testing, 1969.
Cattell, R. B., Eber, H. W., & Tatsuoka, M. M. *Handbook for the Sixteen Personality Factors Questionnaire* (16PF). Champaign, IL: Institute for Personality and Ability Testing, 1970.

Cattell, R. B., & Scheier, I. H. *The meaning and measurement of neuroticism and anxiety.* New York: Ronald Press, 1961.

Eysenck, H. J. *The biological basis of personality.* Springfield, IL: Thomas, 1967.

Eysenck, H. J. *The measurement of personality.* Baltimore: University Park Press, 1976.

Eysenck, H. J., & Eysenck, S. B. G. *Personality structure and measurement.* San Diego: EdITS, 1969.

Eysenck, H. J., & Eysenck, S. B. G. *Manual: Eysenck Personality Questionnaire (Junior & Adult).* San Diego: EdITS, 1975.

Eysenck, H. J., & Eysenck, S. B. G. *Psychoticism as a dimension of personality.* London: Hodder & Stoughton, 1976.

Glasser, A. J., & Zimmerman, I. L. *Clinical interpretation of the Wechsler Intelligence Scale for Children.* New York: Grune & Stratton, 1967.

Institute for Personality and Ability Testing. *Manual for the Early School Personality Questionnaire.* Champaign, IL: IPAT, 1972.

Karson, S., & O'Dell, J. W. *A guide to the clinical use of the 16PF.* Champaign, IL: Institute for Personality and Ability Testing, 1976.

Kohn, M. *Social competence, symptoms and underachievement in childhood: A longitudinal perspective.* New York: Wiley, 1977.

Marks, P. A., Seeman, W., & Haller, D. L. *The actuarial use of the MMPI with adolescents and adults.* Baltimore: Williams & Wilkins, 1974.

Porter, R. B., & Cattell, R. B. *Handbook for the Children's Personality Questionnaire.* Champaign, IL: Institute for Personality and Ability Testing, 1960.

Wakefield, J. A., Jr., Bradley, P. E., Doughtie, E. B., & Kraft, I. A. Influence of overlapping and non-overlapping items on the theoretical interrelationships of MMPI scales. *Journal of Consulting and Clinical Psychology,* 1975, *43*, 851-857.

Wakefield, J. A., Jr., Yom, B. L., Bradley, P. E., Doughtie, E. B., Cox, J. A., & Kraft, I. A. Eysenck's personality dimensions: A model for the MMPI. *British Journal of Social and Clinical Psychology,* 1974, *13*, 413-420.

Wechsler, D. *Manual for the Wechsler Intelligence Scale for Children—Revised.* New York: Psychological Corp., 1974.

Wiggins, J. S. Personality structure. *Annual Review of Psychology,* 1968, *19*, 293-350.

Wiggins, J. S. Personality and prediction: *Principles of Personality assessment.* Reading, MA: Addision-Wesley, 1973.

INDEX

SUBJECT INDEX